INSIDE**OUTSIDE** GUITAR**SOLOING**

Discover Oz Noy's Modern Guitar Soloing Techniques for Rock, Jazz & Blues

OZ**NOY**

With Tim Pettingale

FUNDAMENTAL**CHANGES**

Inside-Outside Guitar Soloing

Discover Oz Noy's Modern Guitar Soloing Techniques for Rock, Jazz & Blues

ISBN: 978-1-78933-227-8

Published by **www.fundamental-changes.com**

Copyright © 2021 Oz Noy

The moral right of this author has been asserted.

All rights reserved. No part of this publication may be reproduced, stored in a retrieval system, or transmitted in any form or by any means, without the prior permission in writing from the publisher.

The publisher is not responsible for websites (or their content) that are not owned by the publisher.

www.fundamental-changes.com

Over 13,000 fans on Facebook: **FundamentalChangesInGuitar**

Instagram: **FundamentalChanges**

For over 350 Free Guitar Lessons with Videos Check Out

www.fundamental-changes.com

Connect with Oz:

Instagram: **oznoyguitar**

Facebook: **oznoymusic**

Cover Image Copyright: Author photo by Mark Seliger, used by permission

Contents

About the Author — 4

Introduction — 5

Get the Audio — 6

Chapter One – The Mixolydian Scale — 7

Chapter Two – The Whole Tone Scale — 27

Chapter Three – The Diminished Scale — 46

Chapter Four – The Altered Scale — 69

Chapter Five – Blending Scale Colors — 93

About the Author

Born in Israel, Oz started his professional career at the age of 13 playing jazz, blues, pop and rock music. By age 16, he was playing with top Israeli musicians and artists. At 24, he was one of the most established guitar players in the country. Oz was also a member of the house band on Israel's top-rated television show for more than two years.

Since his arrival in New York in 1996, Oz has made a huge impact on the local and international music scene. His unique, intoxicating style has broken all the rules of instrumental guitar music by focusing on the groove. Renowned drummers Keith Carlock, Anton Fig, Vinnie Colaiuta, Steve Ferrone, Chris Layton, Dennis Chambers and Dave Weckl have contributed to his recordings, as well as all-star bassists Will Lee, James Genus, John Patitucci, Roscoe Beck and Reggie Washington.

Oz is a prolific recording artist, releasing his debut record, *Oz Live*, in 2001, recorded at NYC's legendary Bitter End. Since then, highlights have included his highly acclaimed studio record, *HA!* with an all-star band featuring Fig, Carlock, Lee and Genus, plus special guests Mike Stern and George Whitty; the 2009 release, *Schizophrenic*, featuring special guest Steve Lukather; *Twisted Blues Vol.1* and *Vol.2*, featuring guests including John Medeski, Eric Johnson, Allen Toussaint, Chic Corea and Warren Haynes; and *Who Gives a Funk?* featuring Joe Bonamassa, Robben Ford, Dweezil Zappa, Fred Wesley, Chris Potter, John Medeski and Corey Glover.

In 2019 Oz released his Boogaloo-inspired album *Booga Looga Loo* and in 2020 released *Snapdragon*, exploring new sonic territory and with guests including Dennis Chambers, Will Lee, Vinnie Colaiuta, Dave Weckl, James Genus, and John Patitiucci and Chris Potter.

For his accomplishments as a trend-setting guitarist, Oz won the highly acclaimed *Guitar Player* magazine readers' poll for "Best guitar riff on a record" (2007), "Best new talent" (2008), and "Best out-there guitar player" (2013).

Oz's success as an artist and instrumentalist has created a demand for him as a teacher. He has released two instructional videos for Jazz Heaven, *Guitar Improvisational Workout* and *Play Along Workout*, and three videos for My Music Master Class entitled *Unlocking the Neck, Blues, Bends and Beyond* and *Effects on the Gig*. He has also created four video courses for TrueFire: *Twisted Guitar: Blues Soloing, Twisted Guitar: Blues Rhythm, Essentials: Funk Rhythm Guitar* and *Improv Wizard*. Oz conducts occasional master classes at The Collective School of Music (New York City), Musicians Institute (Los Angeles), and others.

Oz has toured and recorded with too many artists to name them all here! Highlights include: Chris Botti, Cyndi Lauper, Toni Braxton, Nile Rodgers, Roger Glover, Warren Hayes, The Allman Brothers, Allen Toussaint, Eric Johnson, Mike Stern, John Abercrombie, Steve Lukather, Richard Bona, Gavin Degraw, Nelly Furtado, Natasha Bedingfield, Jennifer Hudson, Don Henley, Patti Austin, Take 6, Michael Bublé, Josh Groban, Phil Ramone, Dweezil Zappa, Steven Tyler, Joe Perry, Sting, Steve Perry, Allison Krauss, Foreigner, Patty Smyth, Idina Menzel, Justin Timberlake, Bonnie Raitt and Dave Mathews.

Introduction

Whenever I teach students, I'm often asked about my *inside-outside* approach to soloing. How do I achieve that outside sound? What am I thinking? Is there a magic formula to it?

It might surprise you to know that I hardly think in terms of "outside" playing at all.

For me, creating tension and resolution in music is all about applying different colors from my harmonic palette. If I play a Mixolydian scale over a dominant 7 chord, that's a relatively inside sounding color. If I use a symmetrical diminished scale over the same dominant 7 chord, that's a bolder choice of color and the music will naturally sound more outside. Both are artistic choices that depend on the context of the music, but there is no magic formula. The magic happens when you have a strong palette of colors to choose from and you know how to apply them in a practical way.

In this book, we're going to look at how we can use different approaches to add outside tension to our solos. We'll begin with the familiar color of the Mixolydian scale. That said, you won't find any routine, clichéd licks here. My aim is to help you break away from predictable patterns and licks and show you how to freshen up your Mixolydian soloing. You'll find yourself breaking new ground with a scale you thought you knew well.

Then we'll move toward the bolder colors of the Whole Tone, Diminished and Altered scales. You'll learn how to use these altered scales to create tension and release in real musical situations, and I'll show you how I handle them over some funky tracks.

For each scale, I'll show you *the most useful* patterns and positions you need to know – the ones you'll return to again and again, because they just work perfectly. I'll also show you some exercises that will help you to embed the sound of the scale in your ears and will create the foundation for composing some cool licks. Then, I'll pass onto you some of the vocabulary I've built around these scales and show you some ideas to help you break out of any ruts you find yourself stuck in.

To complete the journey, we'll end with a performance piece that blends together all the colors we've explored and shows how to apply them over a funky blues. I hope this will inspire you to see what's possible using this approach, and that you will continue to work with the scales in this book, adding the musical ideas to your vocabulary.

Lastly, it's worth mentioning that my musical style has always comprised elements of jazz, funk, rock, blues and R&B, so regardless of what genre you play, there will be ideas here to make you stand out as a player and take you in new directions.

Enjoy your music!

Oz

Get the Audio

The audio files for this book are available to download for free from **www.fundamental-changes.com.** The link is in the top right-hand corner. Click on the "Guitar" link then simply select this book title from the drop-down menu and follow the instructions to get the audio.

We recommend that you download the files directly to your computer, not to your tablet, and extract them there before adding them to your media library. You can then put them onto your tablet, iPod or burn them to CD. On the download page there are instructions and we also provide technical support via the contact form.

For over 350 free guitar lessons with videos check out:

www.fundamental-changes.com

Over 13,000 fans on Facebook: **FundamentalChangesInGuitar**

Tag us for a share on Instagram: **FundamentalChanges**

Chapter One – The Mixolydian Scale

Using scales as colors

When it comes to the relationship between chords and scales, I always think in terms of different scales bringing different *colors* to the music. Diatonic scales produce a certain color, while altered scales produce a whole spectrum of different hues. In this sense, creating music is like composing a painting. We have a blank canvas and we get to decide what colors and tones to bring to it; we decide how much light and shade to add. Instead of thinking in terms of playing "outside", we can think about applying scales that will introduce more dramatic colors to the picture.

In this chapter we're going to use the Mixolydian scale to play over a funky-blues dominant chord vamp. The Mixolydian scale might be familiar to you already, but we'll explore some different ways of working with it that will test how well you know it and create some exciting new sounds. We'll start from the ground up, so that if you've only dabbled with this scale, you'll have a systematic way to learn and use it.

For ease of comparison, I'll teach you all the scales in this book in a C tonality, but we will transpose them to other keys for the performance pieces.

The C Mixolydian scale

C Mixolydian is the fifth mode in the key of F Major and fits perfectly over a C7 chord, which contains the notes C E G Bb. This scale is the go-to for many blues, rock and jazz players. The table below shows its scale notes and intervals.

C	D	E	F	G	A	Bb
Root	2nd	3rd	4th	5th	6th	b7

The scale has the same notes as its F Major parent scale, so some guitarists interpret it as an F Major scale that begins and ends on the note C. However, it's much better to learn C Mixolydian as a scale in its own right. Then you won't fall into the trap of "trying to sound like I'm *not* playing an F Major scale" when soloing!

In order to truly master any scale, you need to understand how its intervals work and how its pattern is laid out across the fretboard. This is the best way to really capture its unique color when improvising. The exercises that follow will greatly facilitate this process.

Let's start by learning the scale, its fretboard geography, and how its intervals work. Then, we will play it in a different key as I show you some Mixolydian vocabulary and explain the thought process behind each lick. At the end of the chapter, all these licks connect together to form a complete solo. By taking a *cellular* approach to learning the phrases, a few bars at a time, you'll be well prepared to tackle the end solo.

Scale positions and shapes

Let's learn to play the scale in two positions – one with the root note on the A string and one with the root on the low E string.

If you're thinking that using just two scale positions sounds limiting, actually the learning process we're about to embark on connects the two positions and opens up the whole fretboard. It also helps to simplify our thinking, so that we're not trying to recall lots of different shapes and positions when soloing.

The chord grids below show the two scale patterns and indicate the location of the root notes, so you can easily transpose them to other keys. I nearly always use these three-note-per-string scale patterns, as I find this the easiest way to access the scale and navigate the full range of the fretboard.

The first pattern has the C root note located on the A string, third fret. The second pattern begins with the C note on the low E string, eighth fret.

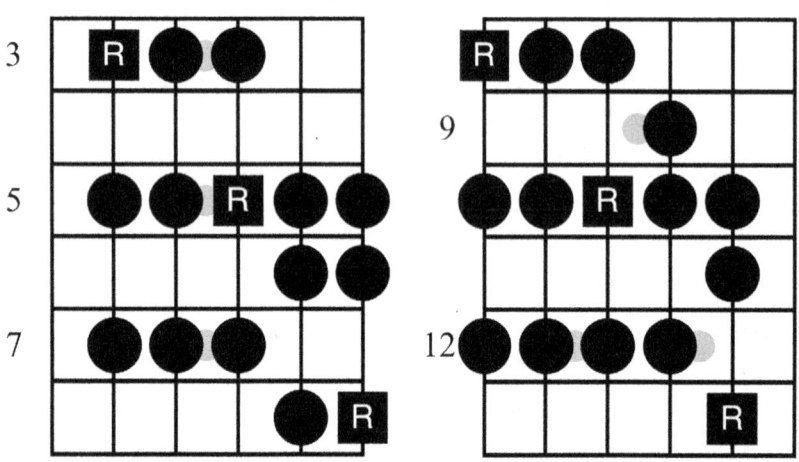

Here is C Mixolydian played ascending and descending from the A string. Play a C7 chord, then play this exercise a few times, listening carefully to how the scale sounds against the chord.

Example 1a

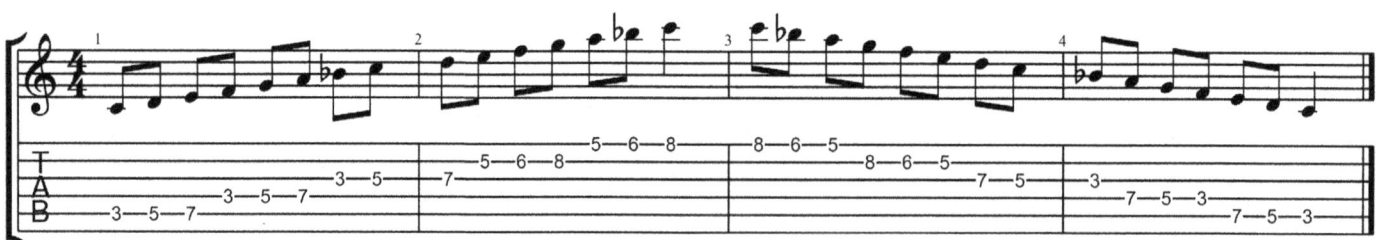

Now play the scale pattern with the root note on the low E string, beginning at the eighth fret.

Example 1b

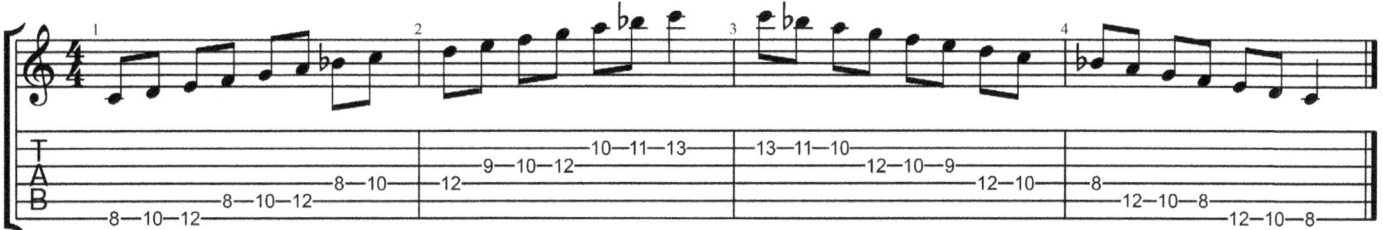

With the sound of the scale in our ears, we're going to take the A string root pattern, and explore a set of exercises that work with the scale both *horizontally* and *vertically* across the neck. This is one of the best ways I know to really *internalize* the intervals so that they become second nature. It's also the route to discovering creative new ideas. Here's why…

Getting the most from the scale

The Mixolydian scale has been used to great effect by many rock, blues and jazz players, and it's very easy to fall back on vocabulary that has been well established by others when improvising. So, how do we create a more contemporary sound and break away from old clichés?

Even with a familiar, "inside" sounding scale like the Mixolydian, which doesn't contain any colorful altered tones like the b9, #9 or #11, by using the *interval sequence patterns* that follow, you'll be able to come up with an endless amount of creative ideas to use for lines.

Working with the intervals in this way is a critical part of the learning process:

- Working creatively with intervals helps us break away from clichéd scale runs and licks
- Playing lines that contain wider intervals makes for less predictable licks
- Using intervallic sequences normally creates a more contemporary sound

These interval patterns in the Mixolydian scale are the ones I use most often in my playing. As well as helping you learn the layout of the intervals on the neck, we'll use an *up-down* sequencing pattern on each one that will help each example sound more like a melodic line and less like a boring exercise.

We'll begin by playing the scale in 3rds, *horizontally* and *vertically*. Then we'll play an *up-down* pattern for both forms.

First, here is C Mixolydian played horizontally (i.e. using the full range of the neck) on the A and D strings. I began in third position and played until I ran out of frets.

Notice in these exercises that I always begin playing a scale from its root, rather than the lowest available note, to get the sound of the tonic in my head. But when descending the scale, I'll often descend past the root in order to use the full range of the position or string group.

Example 1c

Now play through the scale in 3rds again, but this time vertically (i.e. across the strings in the box position).

Example 1d

Now we'll play the 3rds pattern horizontally again, but this time with an *up-down* pattern. This means that we'll alternate between playing an ascending 3rd, going up one scale note, then playing a descending 3rd. Listen to the audio example – once you hear the pattern, you'll get it immediately. This is a great way to make an exercise sound more melodic. Add slides and position shifts wherever you feel most comfortable.

Example 1e

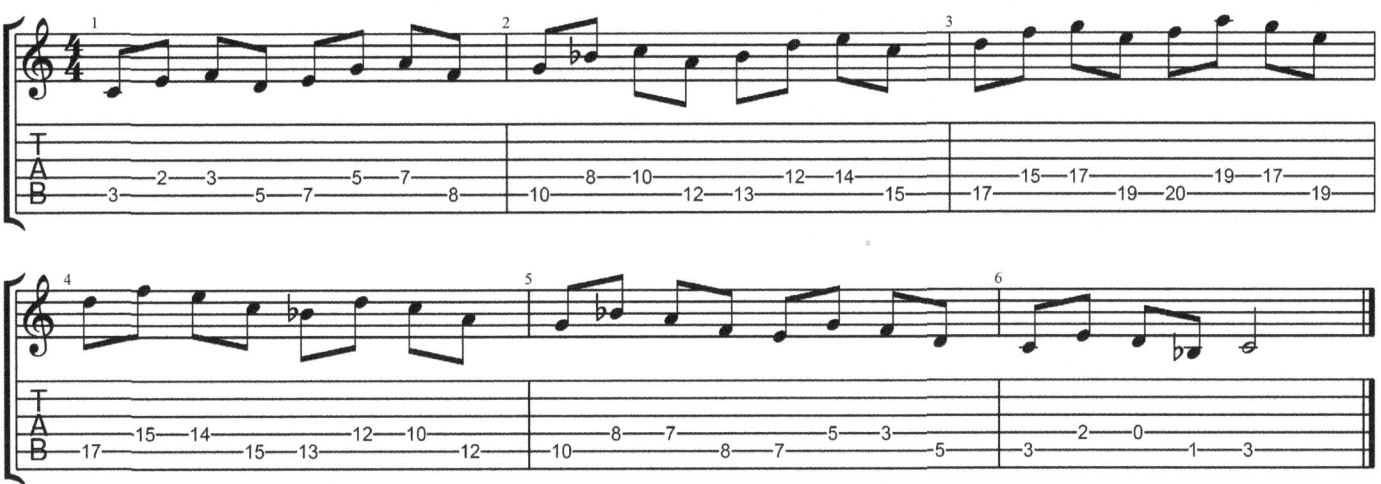

Now we're going to play the same thing, but with the vertical scale pattern.

Example 1f

You can probably already see that this simple exercise will quickly test how well you know any scale. Play the above examples a few times, then see if you can do it without the notation. Your goal is to commit these patterns to memory.

Examples 1a to 1f are your template for learning *every* scale in this book. I won't always spell out both the vertical and horizontal patterns – I'll often show you one, then leave you to work out the other. But from now on, use this as your template for learning any scale. If you work hard at it, the rewards will pay out and you'll quickly develop your own intervallic lines.

For the rest of the intervals in C Mixolydian, I won't show you every permutation, but will focus on key exercises. You should, however, work through all the patterns in your practice sessions.

4th intervals are a key ingredient in the sound of contemporary guitar, and can help us to compose more angular, less predictable sounding lines. Here is C Mixolydian played in 4ths vertically. For self-learning, work out how to play this horizontally.

Example 1g

Now play through the scale in 4ths vertically with the up-down pattern.

Example1h

It's also useful to memorize the scale in 4ths using two-note shapes. These can be used as double-stops when soloing.

Example 1i

Next we'll look at some wider intervals, beginning with 6ths. This is a great interval to have under your fingers, because it is used to create licks in many styles of music. Fortunately, 6ths fall very comfortably on the fretboard.

Here is a slightly different exercise for you to try. We ascend C Mixolydian in 6ths vertically, with an up-down pattern, but descend with regular 6ths.

Since 6ths on the guitar are almost always played with string skips we'll deviate slightly from our vertical scale pattern here for ease of fingering.

Example 1j

13

Now play the 6ths as two-note structures vertically across the strings. Again, these can be used to create double-stop phrases.

Example 1k

The next example uses 7ths horizontally across the neck. 7ths are great for creating spacious sounding lines. You'll also notice that playing 7ths horizontally lets us ascend the neck very rapidly making them a great device for connecting scale positions. Play through this horizontal up-down pattern:

Example 1l

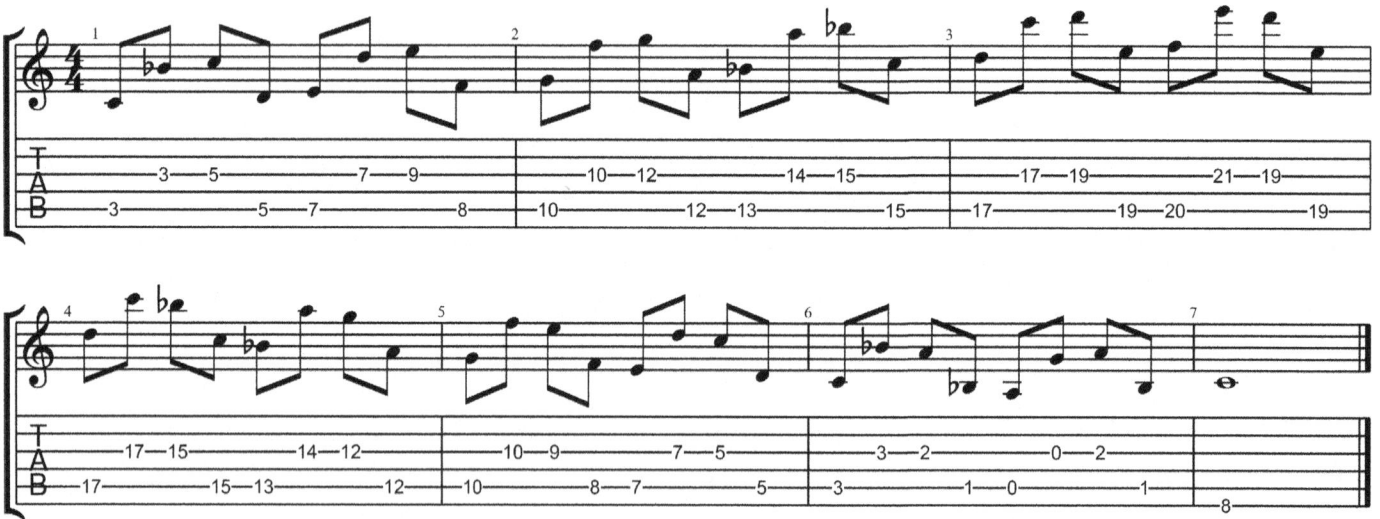

Now let's hear what 7ths sound like played as vertical two-note structures. 7ths are, of course, only one scale step away from each other, but because one of the notes is pushed up an octave, and there is a string in between them, the dissonance is somewhat minimized. They do still sound a little tense when played simultaneously, but in a cool way!

Example 1m

Finally, we can work through the scale in 9ths. I've deliberately missed out 5ths and octaves as they're not as melodic as other intervals, but you should experiment with these during your practice sessions and apply the patterns you've learnt, once you've worked through the higher priority intervals in this book.

The 9th is the second note of the scale but played an octave higher. Added to the upper register of a chord (e.g. Cmaj9, Cm9, C9 etc), it brings a richness to the sound and creates a pleasing tension.

Let's play through the scale in 9ths horizontally.

Example 1n

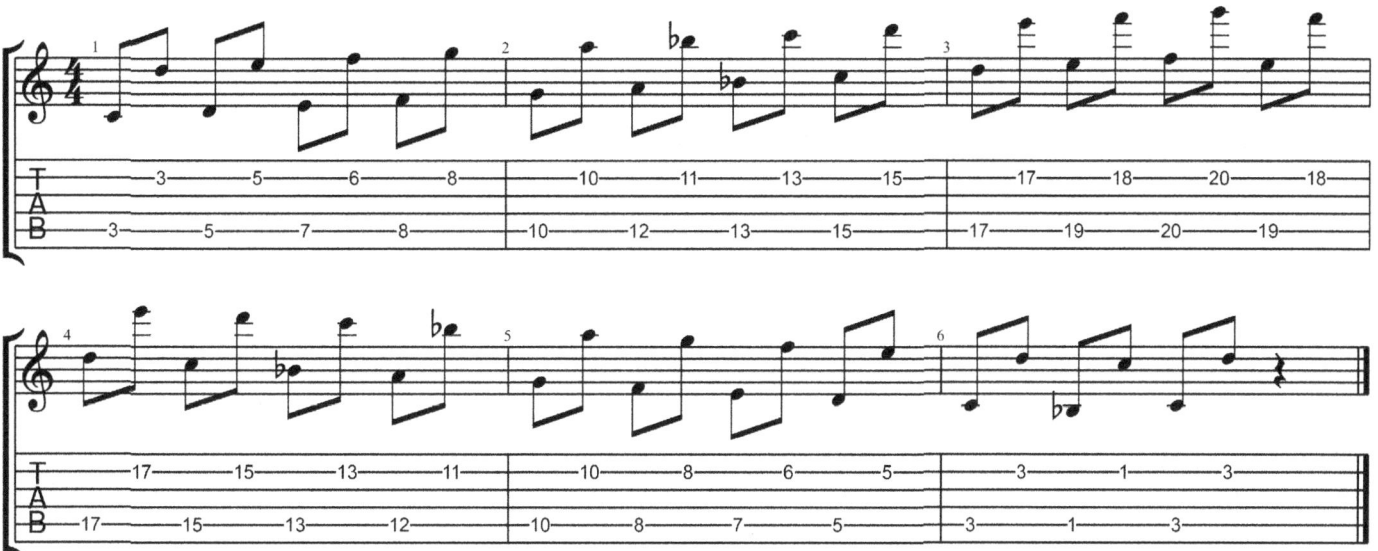

Now try this exercise that uses the horizontal pattern to move through the scale in 9ths. It's more of a challenge to pick this cleanly and accurately with the big string jumps, so learn it slowly before bringing it up to speed. Set your metronome to 60 beats per minute (bpm) to begin with. I recorded the audio example at 90bpm.

Example 1o

Converting the scale to other keys

The three-note-per-string patterns you learnt at the beginning of this chapter provide an easy way to transpose the Mixolydian scale to other keys. The musical examples that follow are based on an A dominant blues vamp – a popular key for blues, rock and funk – so, we need to transpose the scale from C to A Mixolydian.

A Mixolydian is the fifth mode in the key of D Major. Here are the scale notes and intervals:

A	B	C#	D	E	F#	G
Root	2nd	3rd	4th	5th	6th	b7

Using the patterns seen earlier, transposing the scale is simply a matter of locating the root note on the low E and A strings and moving the shape. The E string pattern now has its root note on the 5th fret, and the A string pattern has its root note on the 12th fret.

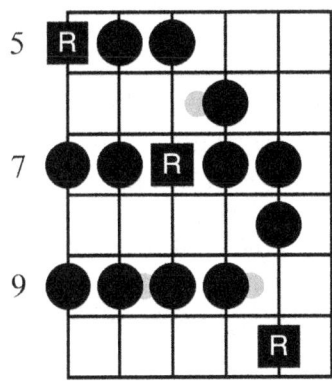 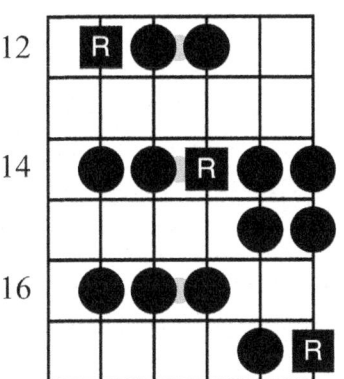

Each key we work with presents different challenges and opportunities when navigating the fretboard. When we were working with the tonal center of C, everything fell quite nicely around the central zone of the neck. Working in A means that we need to repeat the 5th string Mixolydian shape so that we don't ignore the lower register of the guitar.

We can use the exact same A string pattern to cover frets 1-4, using the open strings, as below, to cover the whole neck.

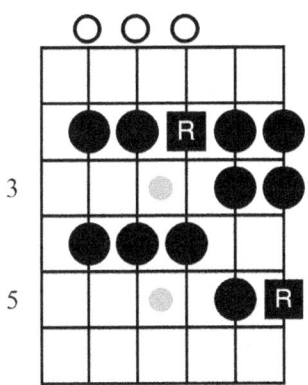

To familiarize yourself with this new key center, follow the practice template laid out at the beginning of this chapter and work through the following process:

- Play through the A Mixolydian scale, ascending and descending, using all three positions
- Play the scale in 3rds, ascending and descending, *horizontally* (i.e. using the range of the neck)
- Play the scale in 3rds, ascending and descending, *vertically* (i.e. using the scale box shape)
- Play 3rds horizontally using the up-down pattern
- Play 3rds vertically using the up-down pattern
- Repeat with the other intervals in the scale (prioritize 6ths, 7ths and 9ths)

This is a significant amount of work, but it will pay dividends if you commit to the process.

Building Mixolydian vocabulary

If you've worked diligently through the process of mastering the scale intervals, you're now ready to learn some vocabulary that will give the Mixolydian scale a new twist. I'll explain each lick as we go and point out any techniques or ideas you need to focus on. At the end, the licks all combine into a full solo etude.

Notice that the examples below are notated in the parent key of D Major (A7 is the V chord in the key of D Major). We'll follow this approach throughout the book, as it will help you to see whenever I'm "coloring outside the lines" (i.e. you'll easily be able to spot any sharp/flat notes in addition to those in the key signature).

We'll begin with some standard bluesy Mixolydian vocabulary to make a strong opening statement to the solo. In bar one, the bend on the high E string is a classic blues approach that targets the 3rd (C#) of the underlying A7 chord. This is a staple sound of Mixolydian vocabulary.

Example 1p

The next example begins to combine some simple intervallic ideas with blues licks. If you continue to practice the intervallic scale exercises covered earlier, you'll find it becomes increasingly easier to compose licks that contain intervallic steps. The idea in bars 1-2 below comes from continuously stacking 3rd intervals, and its effect is to create an "Em7 over A7" sound. Occasionally, I'll add in some chromatic passing notes that approach scale tones from a half step below or above.

Example 1q

At this point I should explain a simple technique I often use to create tension in a solo that I demonstrate in Example 1r. When playing over any chord, I first visualize the "anchor tones", as I like to call them, that define the chord. These are the root, 3rd, 5th and 7th.

These intervals tell you exactly what type of chord you're dealing with. In the case of A7, the anchor tones are the A (root), C# (3rd), E (5th) and G (b7).

If you are aware of these fundamental chord tones that *anchor* down the harmony, then you can play *any* other notes around them, as long as you resolve your line to an anchor tone. For instance, in bar four below, I deliberately play an A# note instead of an A, but flip between the two notes, so it's clear where the "home" sound lies. Look out for this technique as we progress.

Example 1r

Now we begin to move away from blues territory and get more intervallic. We're still using the familiar Mixolydian scale, but the wide interval sequences being used disguise this fact, and make things sound more contemporary. Bar three, for instance, begins with a 6th, then an octave, then a 9th. This is followed by another octave, but with a rest in between to break up the phrase as the line continues. Capturing the rhythmic hook is an important part of this lick, so be sure to listen to the audio example to get it right.

Example 1s

In Example 1t, the line in bar one emphasizes descending 6th intervals. Bars 2-3 contain an example of playing either side of the anchor tones. Scale notes are "enclosed" with notes a whole step above and below. It demonstrates that when you know the scale well, you can become creative with your approach notes.

The final phrase is an example of *sidestepping*. This is a similar technique, whereby we shift a lick up or down briefly, then back to its original location. It's also common to build a sidestep *into* a scale run, so that we begin in the tonic key, shift up or down a half step into another key, then return to the tonic to bring the lick home. Here, I'm shifting between A Mixolydian and Bb Mixolydian. It's a simple but effective way of achieving the inside-outside sound.

Example 1t

The next line begins with more sidestepping and the first three notes are from Bb Mixolydian, a half step above the tonal center of A. You can double your vocabulary by playing Mixolydian patterns a half step away that resolve to the tonal center. This line is designed to grab the listener's attention by not resolving the tension too quickly.

Example 1u

The focal point of the next lick is the 1/16th note triplet run that spans bars 3-4. Although it hints at being an outside line, there is only one "outside note" in the run (the A# in the second triplet group). Keep your hand anchored at the 5th fret and play the notes on the B string as pull-offs. The phrase in the second half of bar four uses approach notes from a half step below to climb back up the scale. The line is based around a typical pentatonic box shape and is similar to the type of ideas Stevie Ray Vaughn would play.

Example 1v

Here is a 1/16th note idea that uses chromatic passing notes to connect the scale tones. Break the first line into four-note blocks and play through them slowly to lock the clusters of notes into muscle memory.

The descending idea in bar two contains only a couple of chromatic notes and yet the line sounds quite outside because I play them on the first and last beats of the bar. Beginning a phrase on an outside note takes the listener by surprise and it takes a moment to adjust the ears and realize that most of the line has the *home* sound.

Example 1w

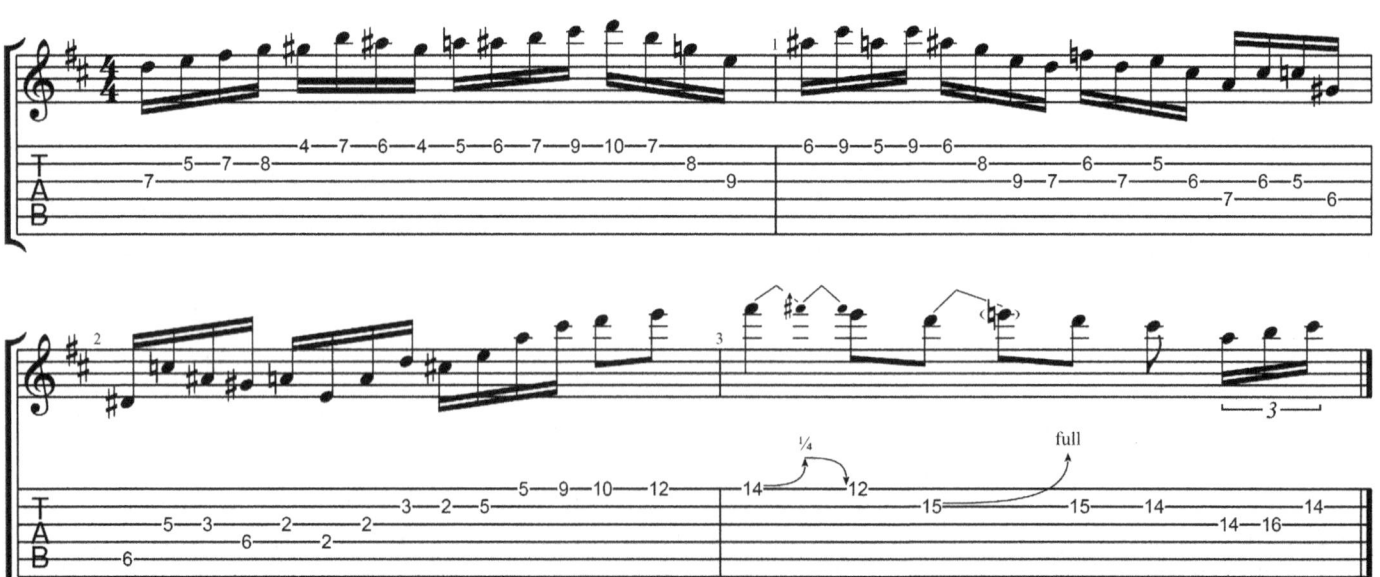

We finish with a challenging 1/16th note run. With a long, complex line like this, the best way to learn it is to slow everything right down and break it into smaller pieces. Focus on memorizing just the first six-note phrase before moving on to the next six notes. Once you have them both down, connect them together and you'll have nailed half of the first bar. Now repeat the process (slowly!) until you're able to connect the entire phrase. Only when you can play it successfully several times without making a mistake should you speed up.

Example 1x

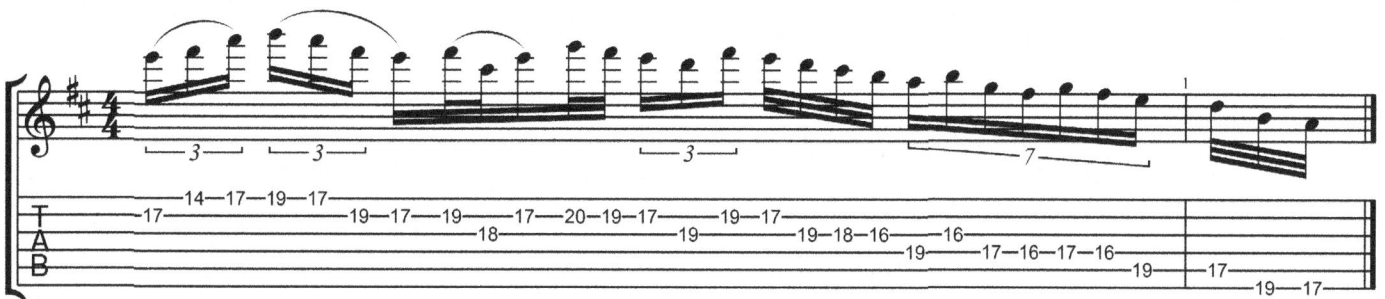

The good news is, you now have every section of the solo under your fingers. Have a listen to the audio to hear the entire solo in context, then begin to work your way through it, connecting together all the cellular licks you've learnt. It'll not only test how well you learnt the phrases earlier, but as you become fluent, you can begin to focus more on your musicality – don't forget to make it groove!

Play the solo along with me a few times, then use this chapter's backing track to play it on your own. You can also use the backing track to jam the ideas we've discussed in this chapter, and to perfect the licks you want to add to your vocabulary.

Example 1y

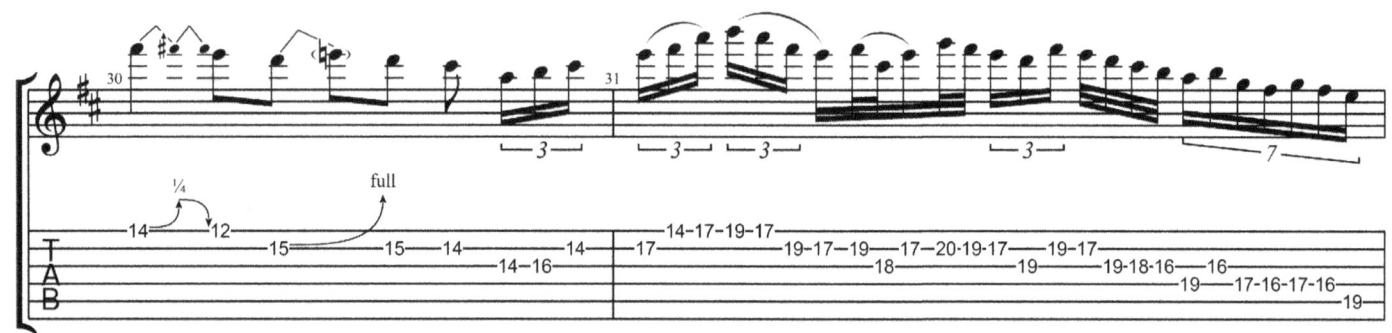

Chapter Two – The Whole Tone Scale

The Whole Tone scale, as its name suggests, is a scale built entirely from whole step intervals. It is a *hexatonic* scale, meaning that there are only six tones per octave. Its perfectly symmetrical shape means it has an ambiguous sound – like it's searching for a destination but never arriving. This makes it very useful for adding an exciting altered color to our solos, from which we can always bring the sound *home* by resolving to a chord tone or "inside" sounding lick.

A triad built on any note of the Whole Tone scale is always augmented, and the entire scale can be expressed by playing two augmented triads a major second apart. This makes it especially useful for playing over dominant chords, as we'll see below.

In jazz, many players heading in a modal direction have incorporated whole tone ideas into their playing, but I also find it very effective in a blues-rock and funk context. In this chapter, you'll get to grips with the scale by playing it over a funky blues in C.

The C Whole Tone scale

To understand how the Whole Tone scale functions over a dominant chord, let's compare it to the C Mixolydian scale from the previous chapter. Here's a reminder of the notes/intervals of C Mixolydian:

C	D	E	F	G	A	Bb
Root	2nd	3rd	4th	5th	6th	b7

Now, here are the notes of C Whole Tone and the intervals it highlights when played over a C7 chord.

C	D	E	Gb	Ab	Bb
Root	9th	3rd	b5	#5	b7

C7 is constructed: C (root), E (3rd), G (5th), Bb (b7). The effect of playing C Whole Tone over C7 is to imply the following altered sounds:

- C7#11 sound (C, E, F#, Bb)
- C7b5 (C, E, Gb, Bb)
- C7#5 sound (C, E, G#, Bb)
- C7b13 (C, E, G, Bb, Ab)

In addition to its altered tensions, the C Whole Tone scale contains a D note, which when played over C7 creates a C9 sound.

As in the previous chapter, we'll begin by learning how this scale is laid out on the fretboard and I'll show you the two main positions I like to use for it. Next, we'll get familiar with how its intervals work through a series of exercises, before learning some of my vocabulary.

Because of its symmetrical shape, with equally spaced intervals, there are a few different approaches to playing this scale, but I have found the following shapes to be both economical and easy to navigate. Here are the A string root and low E string root shapes.

Note that for the A string root shape, I've added the scale notes on the low E string to complete the pattern (indicated by hollow notes). Doing this means that both shapes now have a 3 2 3 2 2 3 note-per-string pattern.

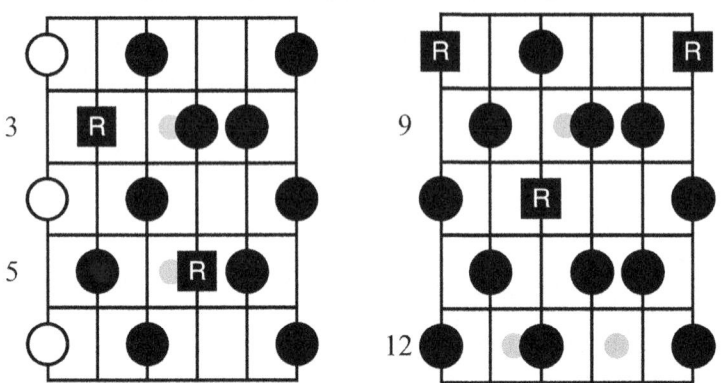

Play a C9 chord, then play through the third position scale shape that begins on the A string root. You can add in the notes on the low E string when you're comfortable with the shape. Make a loop of the C9 chord to play along to, or practice over the C Whole Tone backing track that accompanies this chapter.

Example 2a

Now play through the scale in the higher register with the root note at the 8th fret.

Example 2b

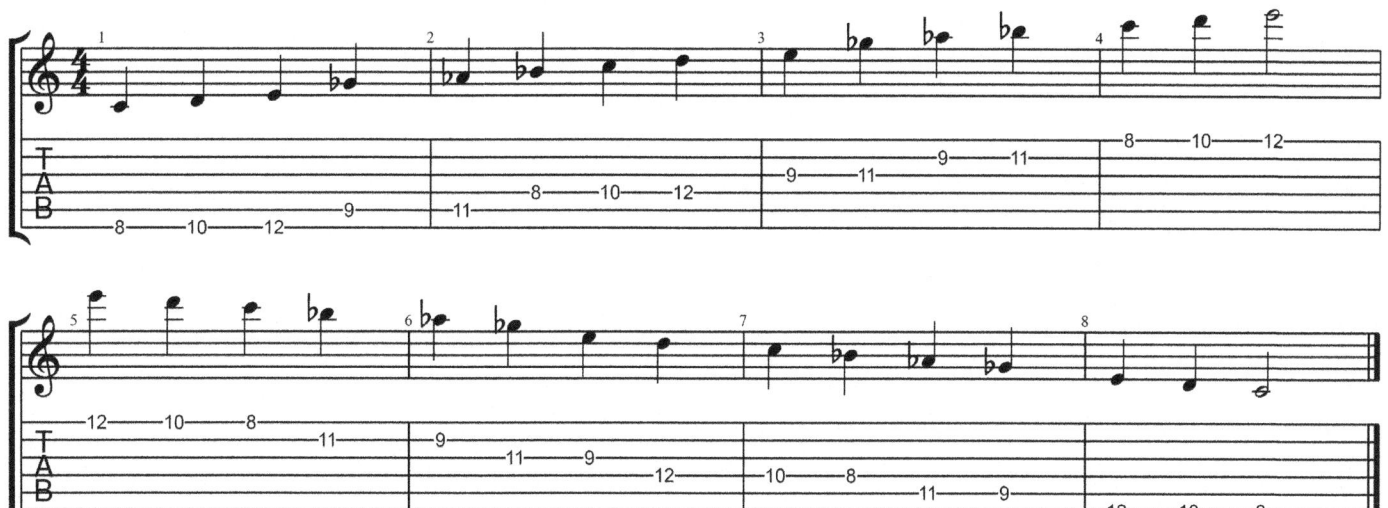

Now we will work through a set of exercises similar to those in Chapter One. Remember, the goal of these exercises is to:

- Enable us to work creatively with the scale intervals
- Play less predictable melodic lines that have wider intervals
- Build intervallic sequences that produce a contemporary sound

As before, we'll learn some horizontal and vertical patterns, which will connect the two scale positions above and give us good coverage of the entire fretboard.

Example 2c is the C Whole Tone scale played in 3rds, moving horizontally across the neck on the A and D strings. You can, of course, learn the scale horizontally on other string pairs, but this is the approach I tend to use to connect lower and higher scale shapes, beginning on the A string root.

Example 2c

Notice the cascading sound of this scale. It has an ethereal quality to it and even when we land back on the C note, it still doesn't really sound resolved.

Here is how you can play the scale in 3rds using the vertical arrangement. Practice this ascending and descending.

Example 2d

Next, we're going to play the scale in 3rds vertically across the neck using the one-up one-down pattern. Because this scale has an unusual pattern, once you've memorized the shape of the exercise, try to play it without the notation and rely solely on the sound of the intervals. This will help to embed it in your ears as well as training your muscle memory.

Example 2e

The next exercise, this time played in 4ths, is a good example of how we can use intervallic patterns to transition between lower and higher positions.

Example 2f

Here is a similar exercise, played in 4ths with the one-up one-down pattern.

Example 2g

The next exercise will test your ability to play cleanly, as well as your ability to hear wider intervals. Normally, 5ths are easy to play on guitar, but since we're dealing with the Whole Tone scale, things are not quite as predictable. It demands some string skipping and quick fretting hand position changes. What feels comfortable for me, might not be comfortable for you, however, so work through this slowly, internalize the sound of the intervals, and work out the most economical and comfortable fingering.

Example 2h

Next, we move on to exploring the scale in 6ths. Through the following three exercises, we'll play the scale as straight intervals, then with an up/down sequence, and finally as double-stops.

Example 2i

Here's C Whole Tone in 6ths, with the one-up, one-down pattern.

Example 2j

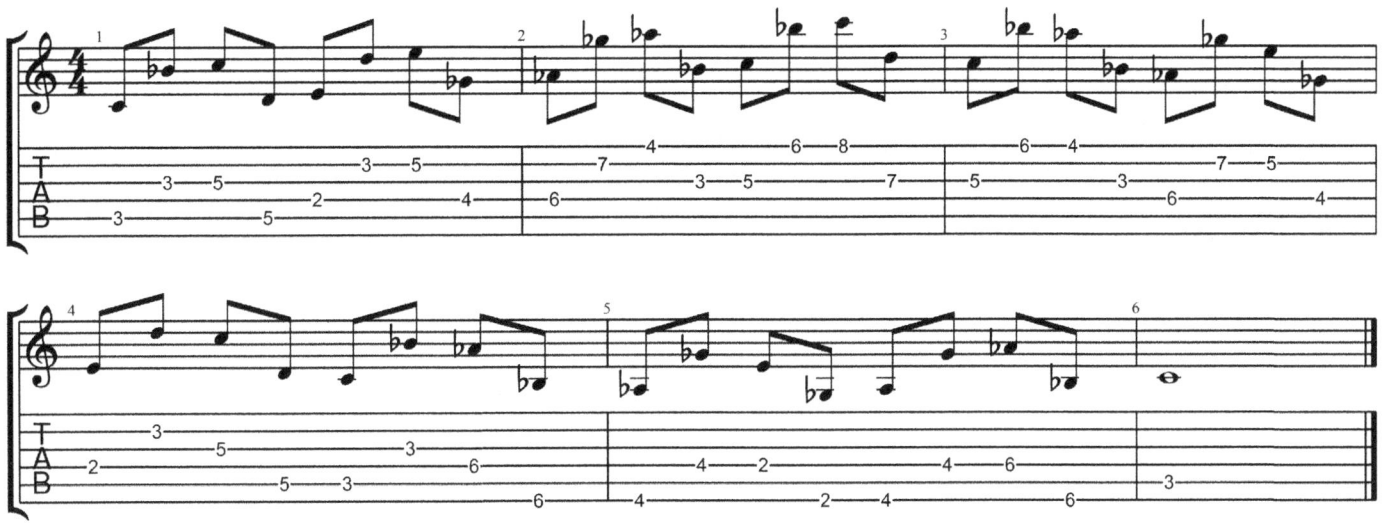

And played as double-stops.

Example 2k

Building Whole Tone vocabulary

Now we'll move on to learning how to apply the Whole Tone scale in a musical context. As before, you'll learn these phrases in two- or four-bar cells – each of which connect to form the complete solo. The work you put into practicing these individual phrases will make tackling the full solo much easier.

The solo is based on a C dominant groove. The overall vibe I wanted to capture here was a strong blues feel, but with plenty of twists and turns. The Whole Tone scale can deliver this in spades. The first example sets the tone with some standard bluesy vocabulary in bars 1-2. This is followed by a Whole Tone run built mainly from 3rd intervals.

Example 2l

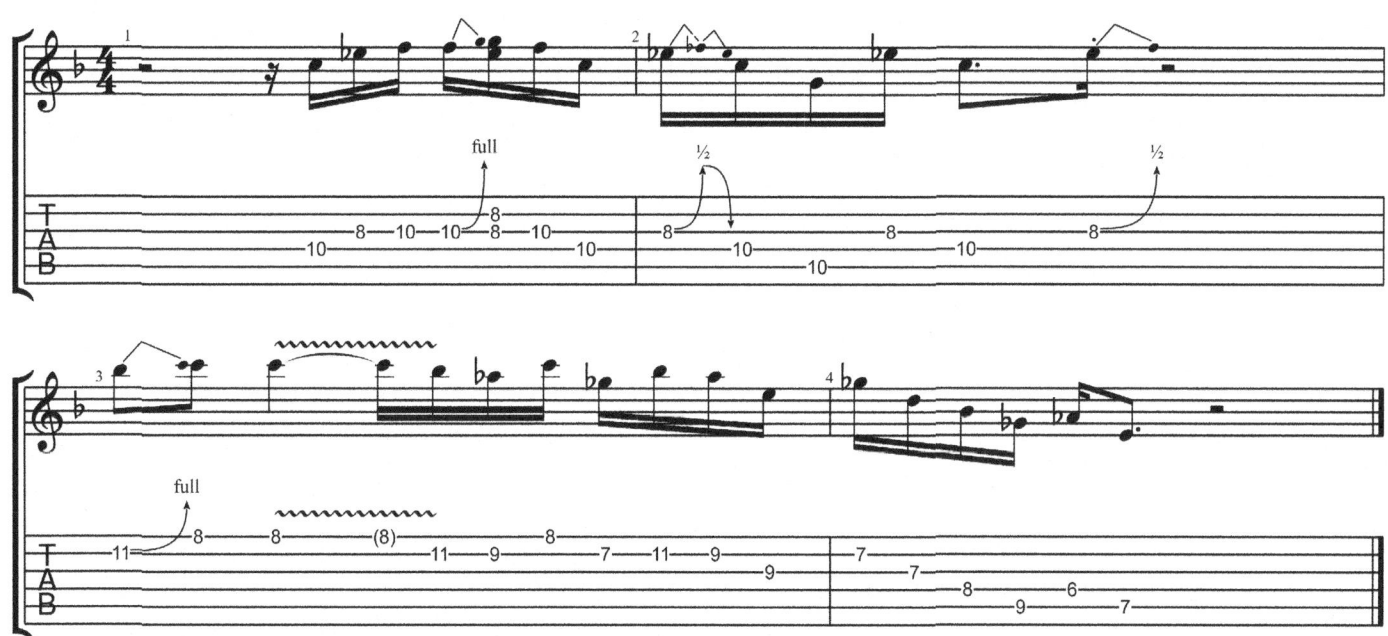

It's important not to overuse altered scales and force that color constantly throughout our solos. If we do, our audience will quickly lose sight of the harmony. Plus, it can detract from the surprise effect of when we *do* use it.

In the next example, I use mostly C minor pentatonic vocabulary for the whole lick, apart from the penultimate note. That Gb note from C Whole Tone introduces the intervallic lick you'll learn in Example 2n.

Example 2m

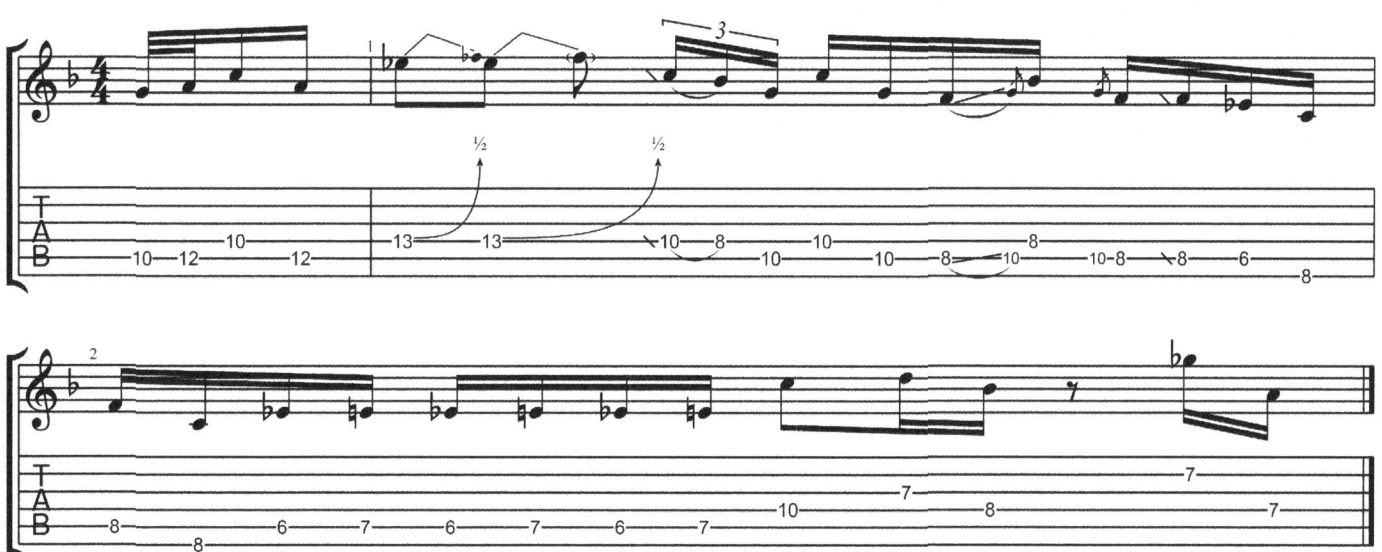

This lick uses wide intervals to create a spacious sound. Taken out of context it might sound a bit random, but combined with the previous idea it's an aggressive, attention-grabbing line that dovetails well with the blues vocabulary.

This line also makes use of the symmetrical pattern of the Whole Tone scale on the guitar neck. Look back at the scale shape diagrams and you'll notice that the pattern of notes on the high E string is identical to that on the D string; and the pattern on the B string matches that of the A string. This means that when we are playing on the B and high E strings, it's easy to visualize big jumps like the ones in this lick.

Example 2n

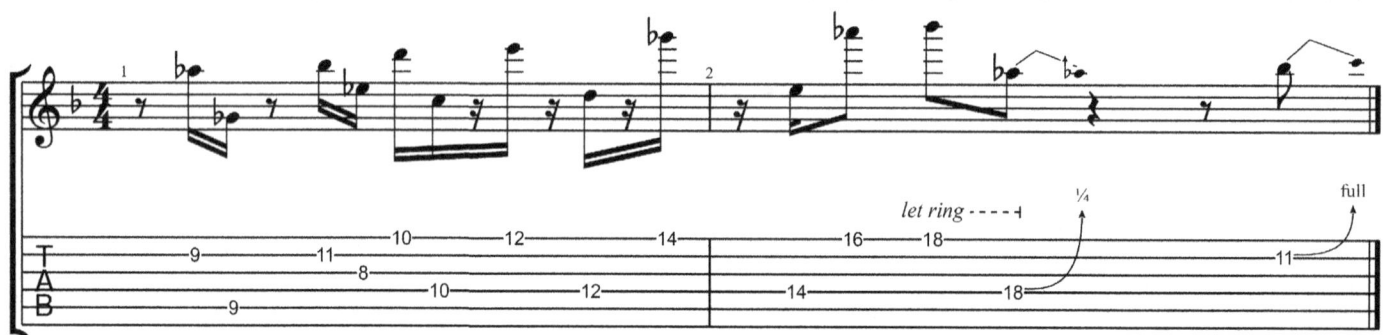

The next example features one of the trickiest inside-outside lines in the entire book! This is not only because of its speed, but also its rhythmic complexity. To learn it, I recommend the following approach:

First, slow things right down. It's important to lock the shapes and hand movements into muscle memory.

Second, learn it in manageable chunks. I suggest breaking bar one in half and learning it as two distinct phrases, before joining them together. Learn the long, mostly 1/32nd note line, as one phrase, and the two triplet figures at the end of bar one as the second phrase.

Repeat this approach in bars 2-3 by learning the four triplet figures at the beginning of bar two as one phrase, and the remainder of bar two/bar three as the second phrase.

Pay special attention to the rhythms throughout. Once you've got the individual phrases down, you can work at connecting them together into one long line.

The line itself weaves between C Mixolydian and C Whole Tone scale notes.

Example 2o

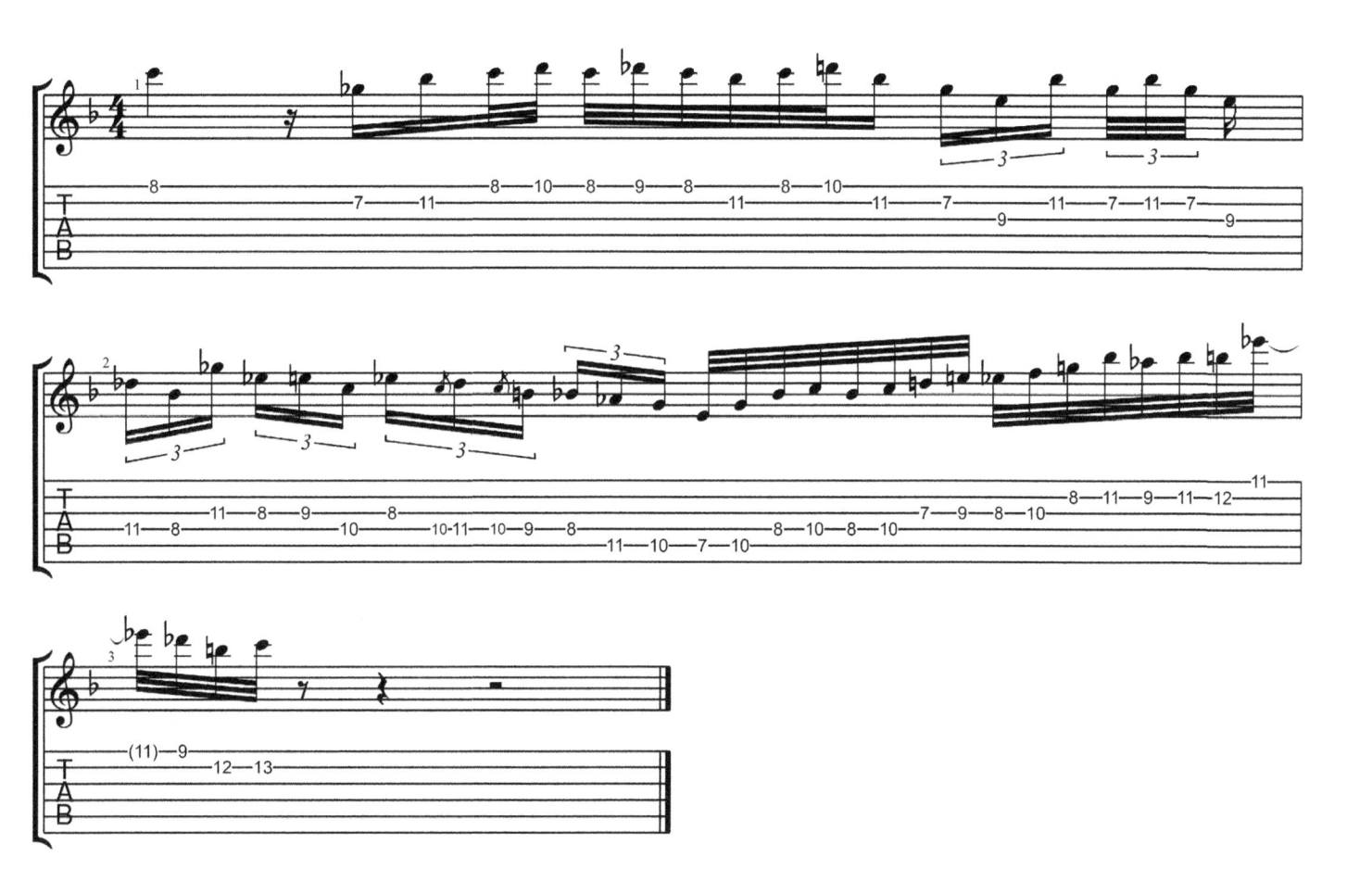

To provide contrast to the previous idea, the next line begins with some blues vocabulary in the pickup bar and bar one. This is followed in bar two by a pure Whole Tone run constructed from 3rds. If you play those notes together, you'll see that they form an augmented chord shape.

Example 2p

This line begins with a three-note phrase that spells out an augmented triad. The second phrase is another augmented triad, preceded by a lead-in note. It's worth studying the line that crosses the end of bar one into bar two closely, as it demonstrates a simple way to "ground" a Whole Tone lick by morphing it into a blues phrase.

Example 2q

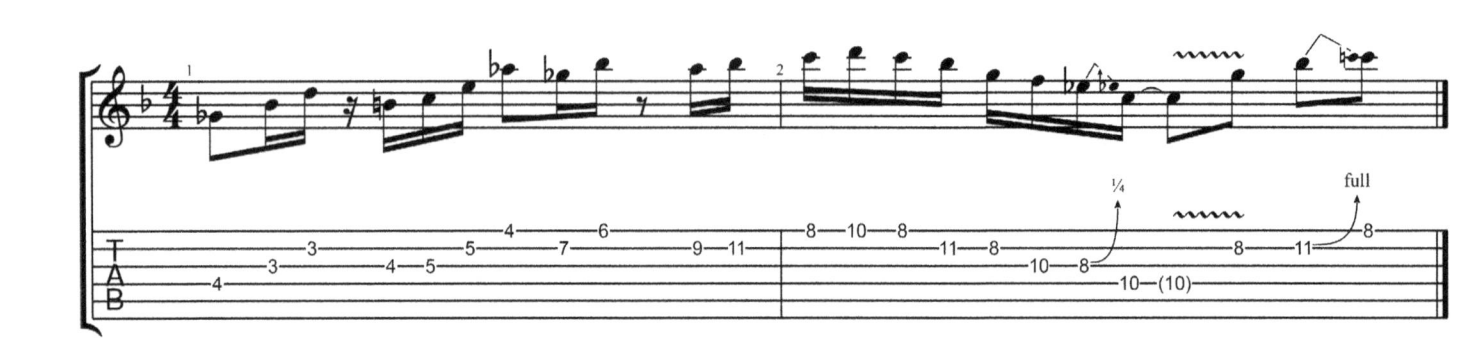

Flipping this idea around, here's an example that begins with a bluesy lick that morphs into a Whole Tone phrase.

Example 2r

Here's another line that brings out the augmented sound of the scale with a descending rhythmic motif. In bar four, the descending figure that begins with a Gb note on the B string, fret 7, spells an Ab7#5 chord and highlights the augmented (#5) quality of the Whole Tone.

Example 2s

It's possible to do some wild stuff with the Whole Tone scale when using it to play double-stops or chord fragment ideas. This next lick pushes the boundaries of this altered scale to create tension.

For the riff-like phrase in bar two, mute the strings in between the low and high notes, just as you would if you were playing an octave. To achieve this, fret the notes on the A and D strings with your middle and ring fingers respectively, and allow your pinkie to rest lightly on the strings, tucked behind them. This will mute the G and B strings and allow the notes on the high E string to ring out.

Lots of tension occurs in bars 3-4 as these notes are only one scale step apart, deliberately creating a dissonant color. To play these double-stops accurately, fix your fretting hand into position, then just focus on aiming for the highest note in each structure. This way you're only thinking about targeting one fret at a time instead of two.

Example 2t

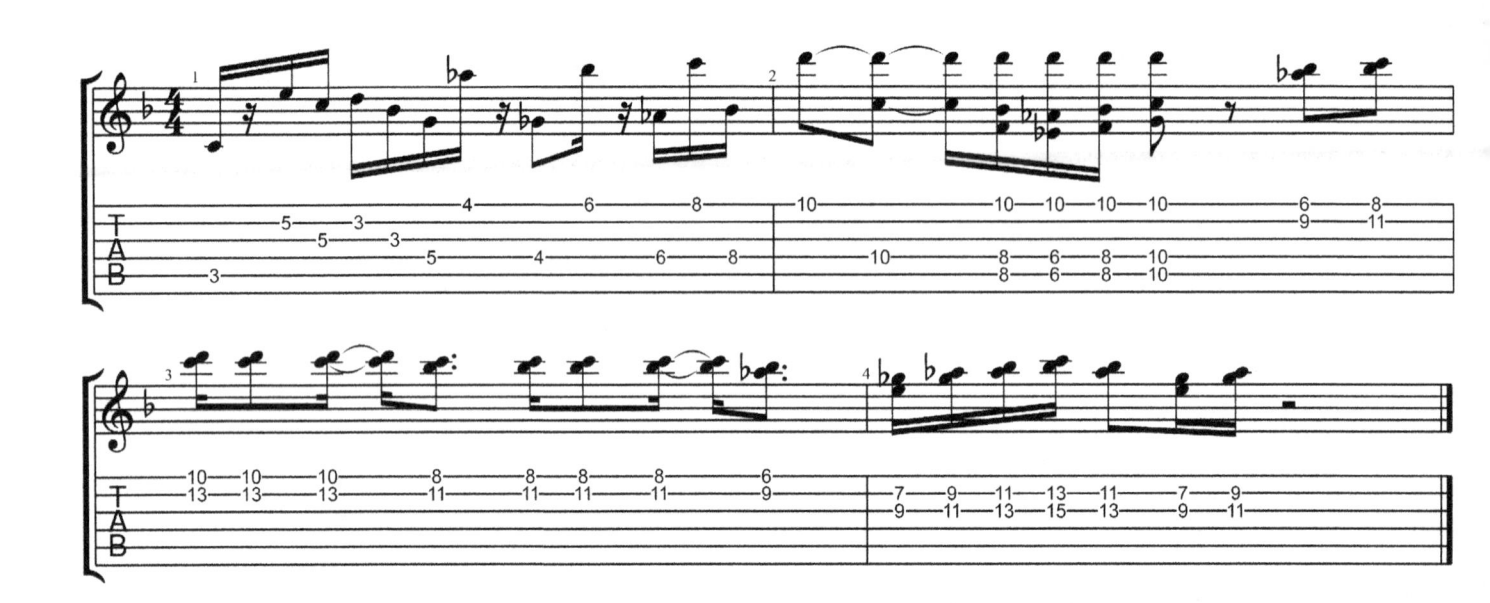

This lick combines blues licks with a standard pentatonic phrase at the end, which has one chromatic note added.

Example 2u

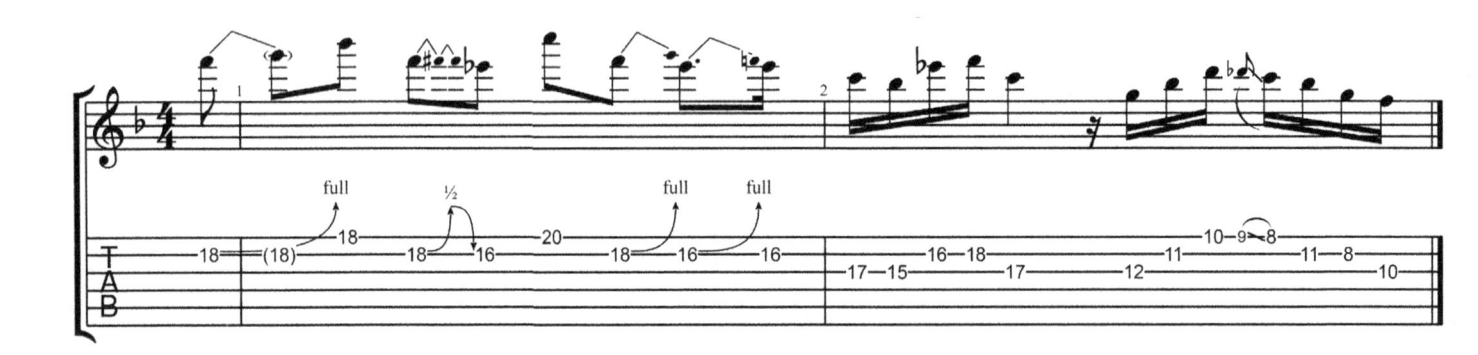

The final lick, while not as hard to play as some of the earlier runs, has a lot going on harmonically, with plenty of twists and turns. It is a motif-based idea, developed across several bars. After opening with some blues vocabulary, the motif statement begins at the end of bar one and crosses into the next bar. The rhythm of this phrase is repeated throughout bars 2-3 and the motif repeats, moving up a whole step each time to produce some outside tension.

Example 2v

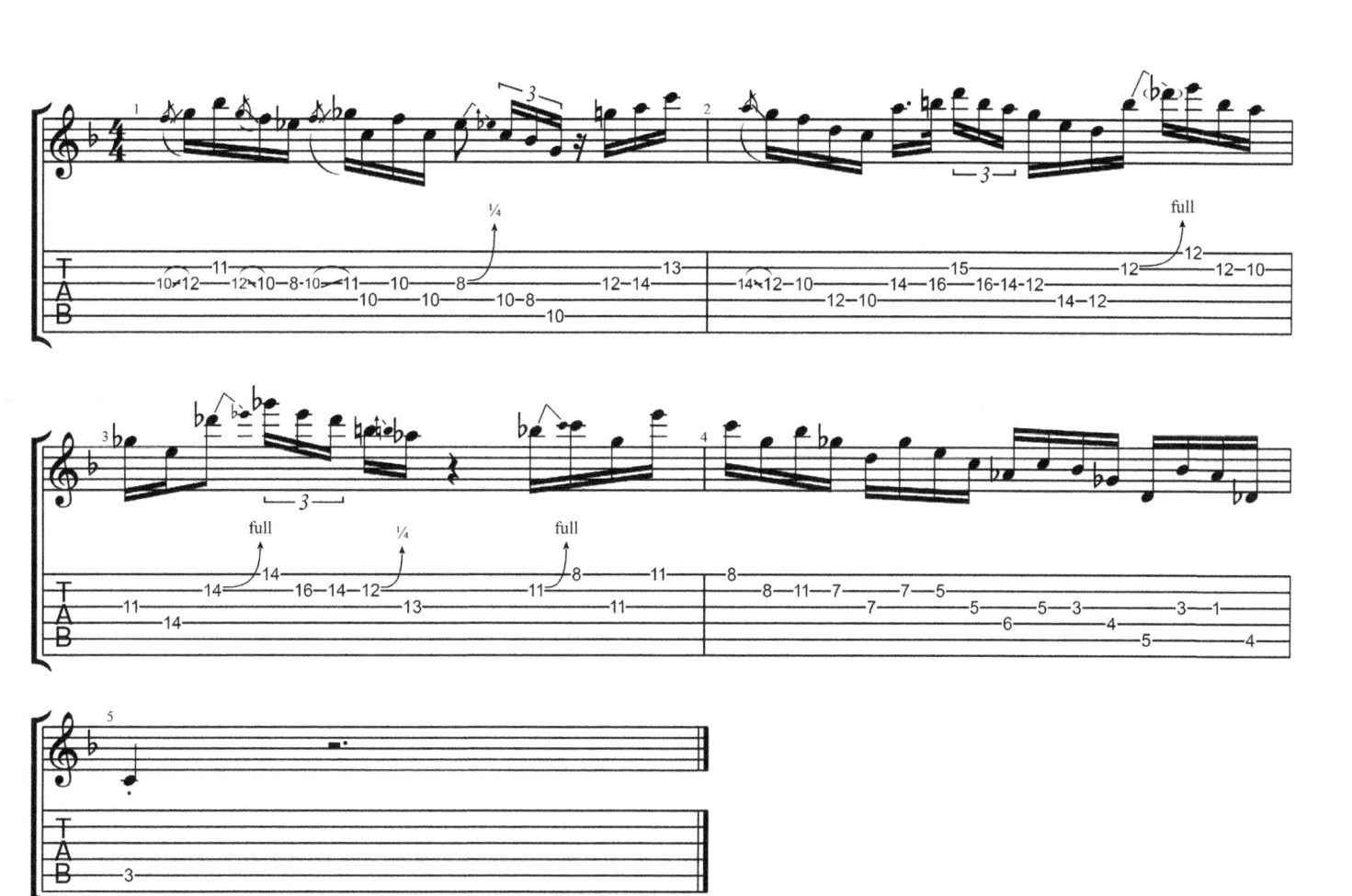

After you've worked to master the individual licks in this chapter, it's time to tackle the full solo. You'll notice that some of the phrases you've learnt appear in slightly different places in the bar. In a couple of the previous examples, I wanted to teach you entire phrases that made musical sense on their own, hence some of them were written with pickup bars. Listen to the audio performance a few times before you begin.

Example 2w

42

43

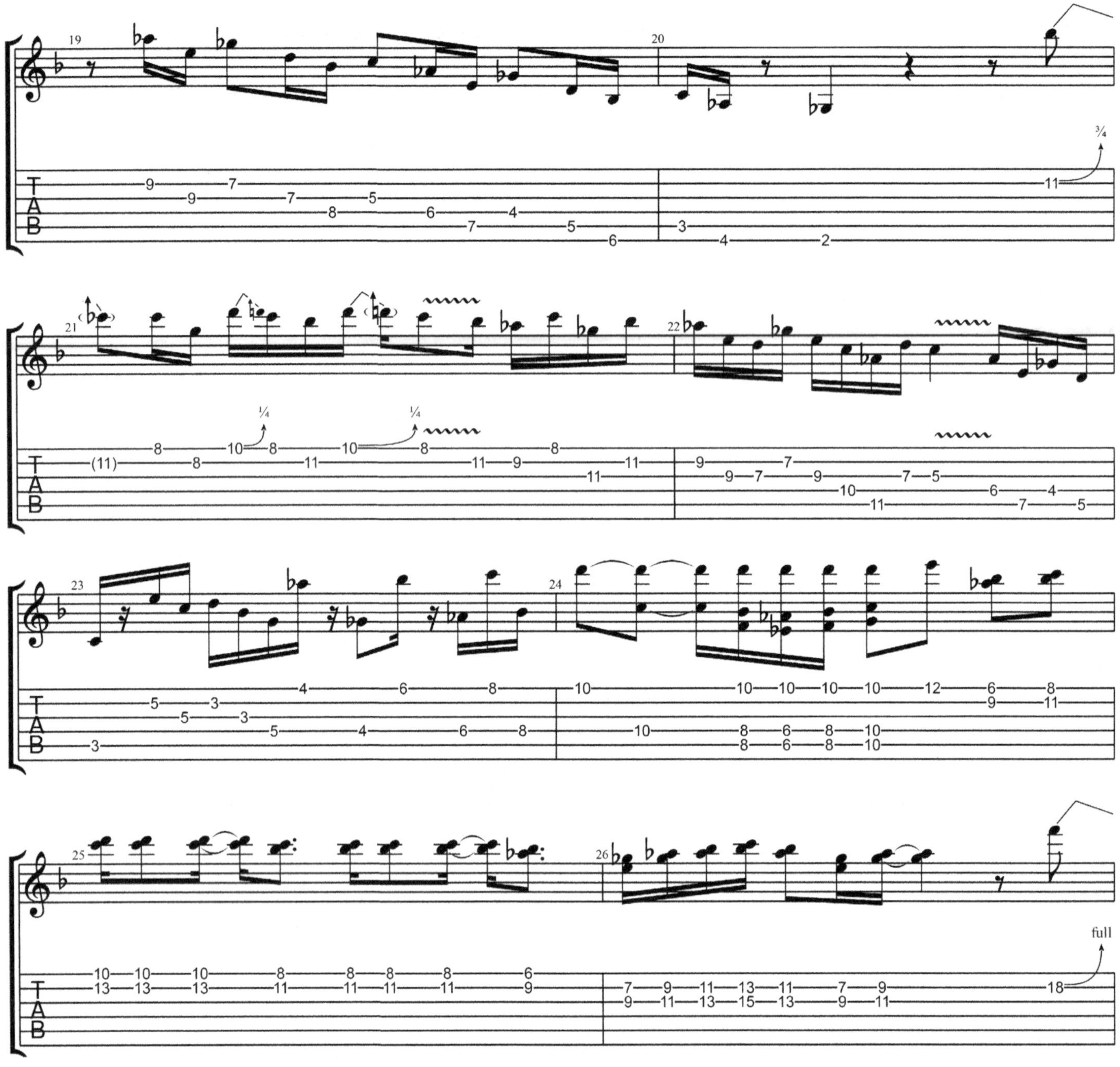
3/4
1/4
1/4
full

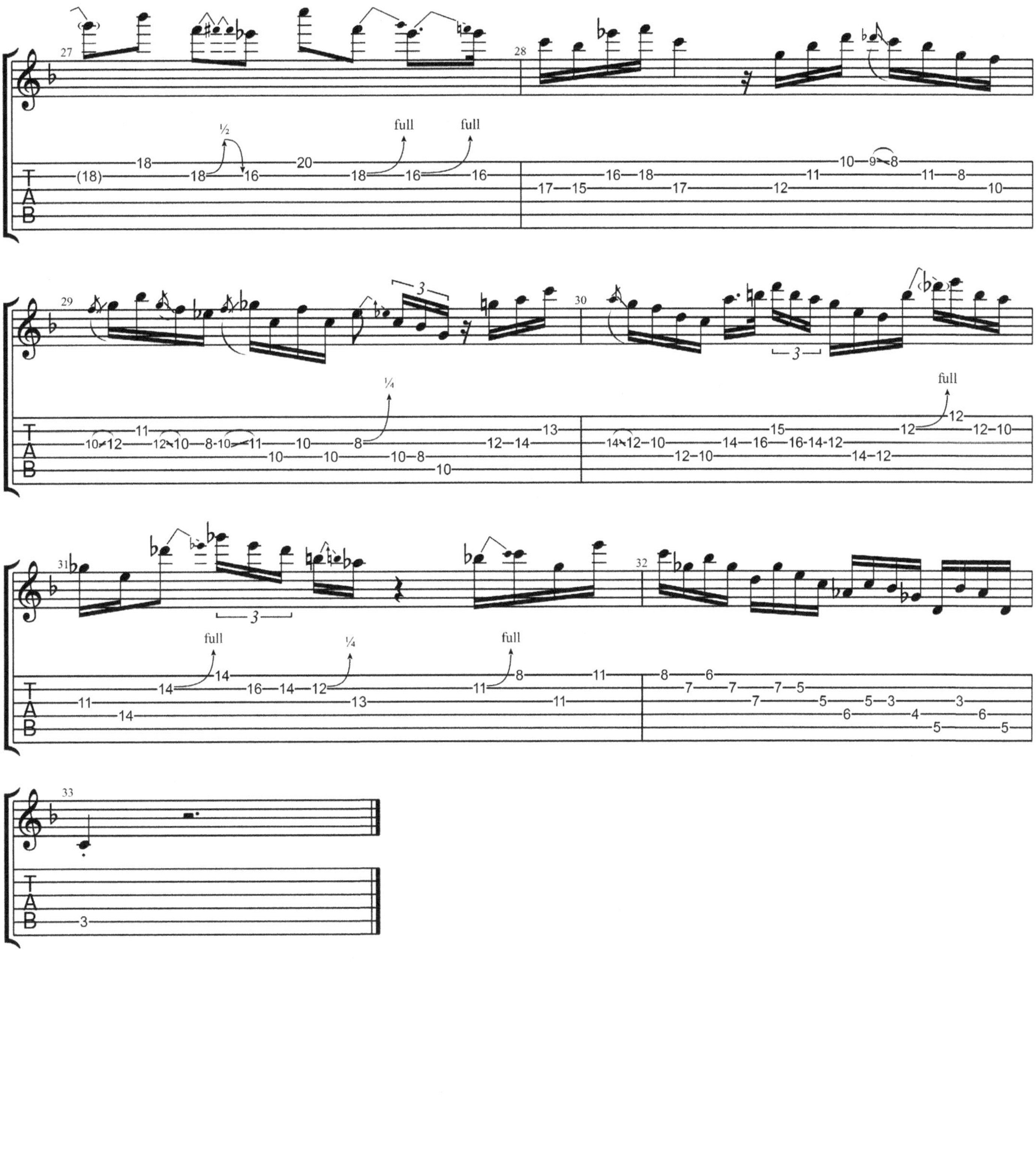

46

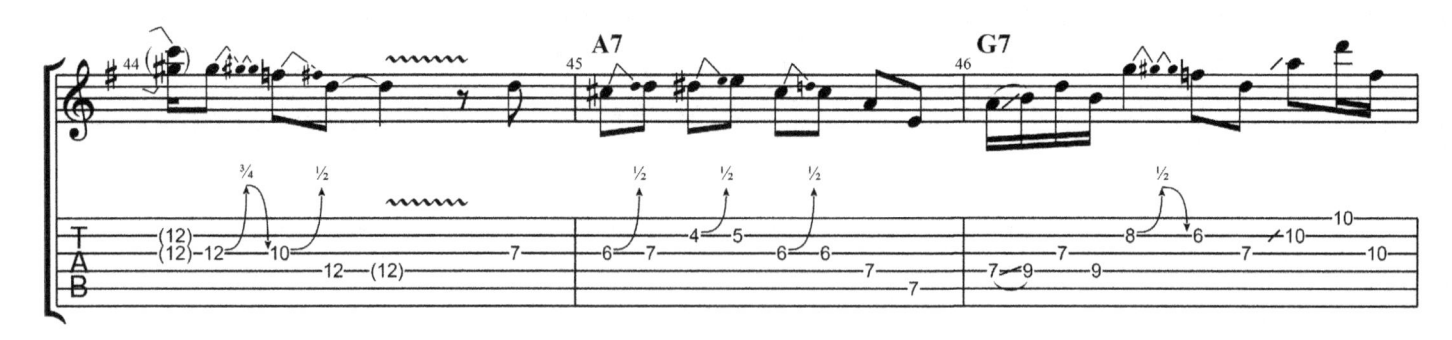

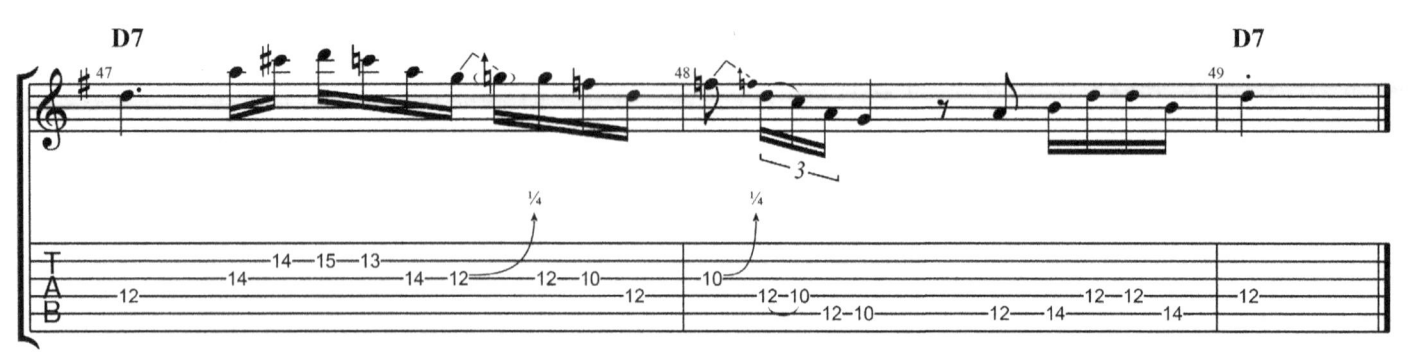

Chapter Three – The Diminished Scale

The next color we're going to use to create inside-outside lines is the Diminished scale. I think of the Diminished as producing a darker color than other altered scales, and it contains some interesting tension notes that will challenge your ears if you're not used to hearing them. It is perhaps the jazziest sounding of the scales we're looking at and has been used extensively by musicians such as John Coltrane and Allan Holdsworth.

Whenever I teach Diminished scale vocabulary to students, I often find I need to take a step back and explain in basic terms what the scale is and how it's formed. There seems to be a lot of confusion about this scale, not least because there are several different names for it, all of which describe the same thing from a different viewpoint (e.g. Half-Whole Diminished, Whole-Half Diminished, Dominant Diminished, etc).

Here is an easy way to form the diminished scale and to know how to apply it. This is the rule jazz musicians use to quickly locate and play the diminished sound over any dominant chord:

Play the diminished scale a half step above the root of a dominant chord.

For example, over a C7 chord, we play the C# Diminished scale.

Let's take a look at why this rule works. Someone has said that a diminished chord is just a "dominant chord in disguise". Here's why…

Take a look at the C# diminished chord diagram below. You're probably familiar with this common moveable shape for playing it, which has the root note on the high E string.

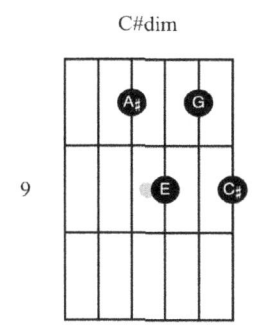

If we add a C root note to this shape on the low E string, it transforms into a C7b9 chord:

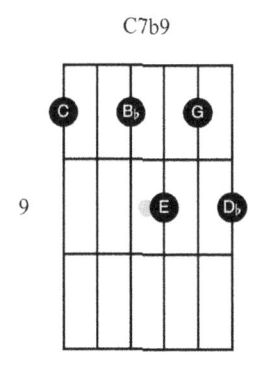

47

This is the diminished-dominant connection and why a diminished chord is so closely linked to a dominant chord.

Now let's look at how to form the correct scale to play over the C altered dominant chord we've just created. Our starting point is the arpeggio of the C#dim7 chord. Below is an easy way to play it from its root note on the A string, fret 4.

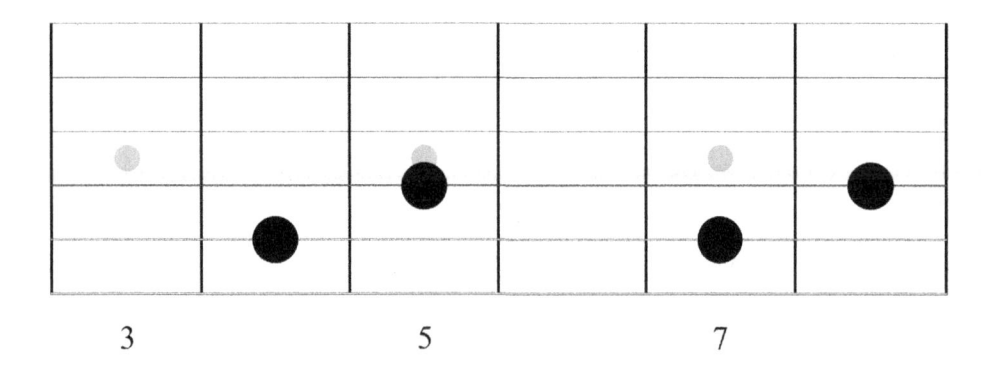

If we add a note a half step below each C#dim7 arpeggio note, we get all eight tones of the C# Diminished scale. Here's how the scale shape looks (with the notes we're adding indicated by hollow circles).

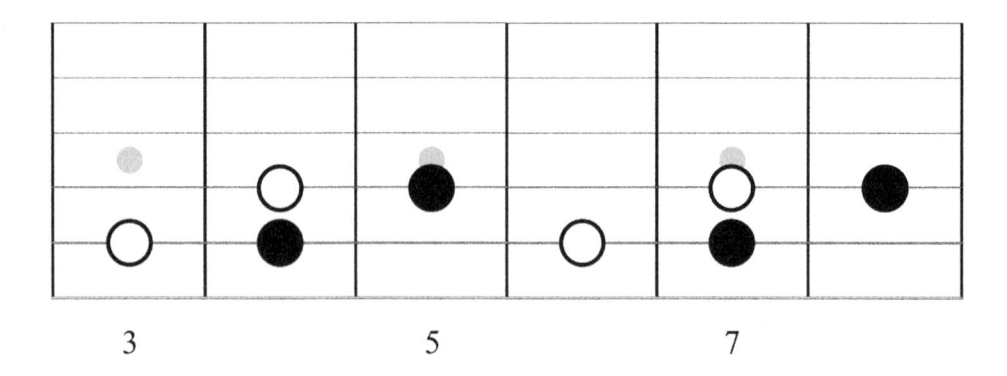

We now have a useful shape for the C# Diminished scale that begins on the root note of the C7b9 chord.

As with other altered scales, we can simply play it over a straight C7 chord. The table below shows the intervals that are highlighted when we play the above pattern over C7.

C	Db	D#	E	F#	G	A	Bb
Root	b9	#9	3rd	#11	5th	13th	b7

The scale contains all the chord tones of C7, an extended 13th (A) note, and b9 (Db), #9 (D#) and #11 (F#) tension notes – the #11 being the most outside sounding tension.

Having formed the correct scale to play over a C dominant chord, we now need to practice it from the C root note. As you'll know by now, I always prefer to *think from the root* of the chord I'm playing over.

There are several useful shapes for this scale. We'll begin with some box shapes, then look at some crawling patterns that are useful for spanning the fretboard. Shape 1 is a three-note-per-string vertical shape with an A string root. The root notes are indicated below, so that you can easily transpose this shape to other keys.

Shape 1

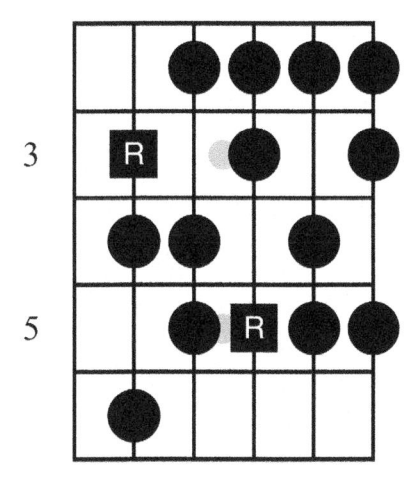

Play a third position C7b9 chord, then play through the scale and listen to the sound of the intervals over the chord.

Example 3a

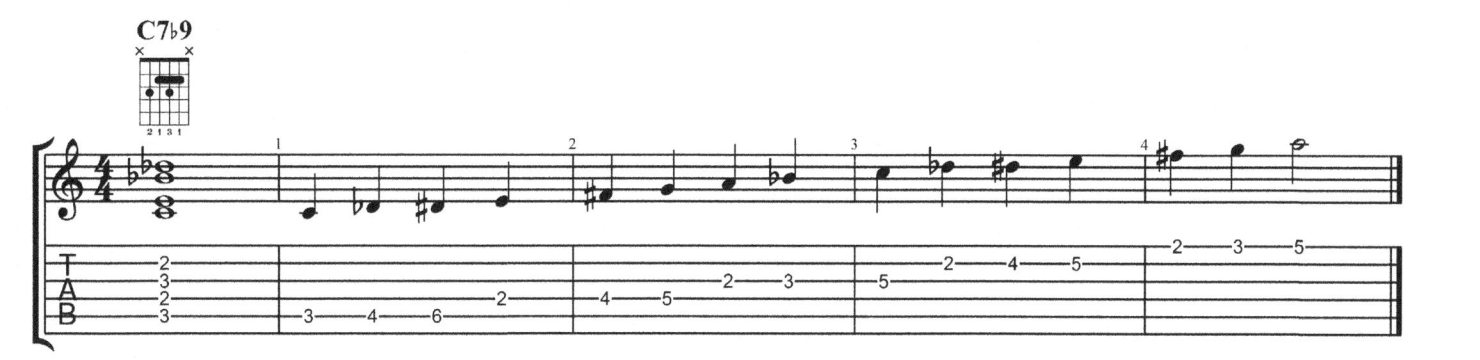

The next three-note-per-string shape has a root on the low E string. Play the C7b9 chord, then play through the scale ascending and descending.

Shape 2

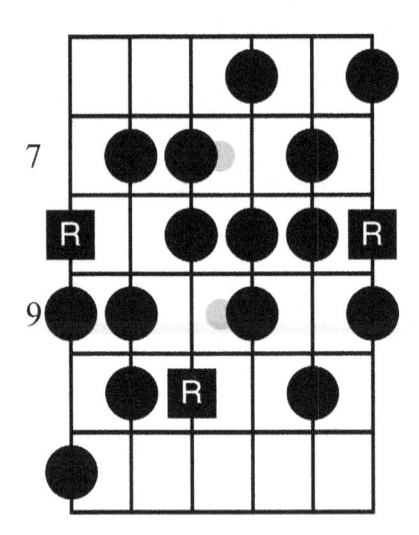

Example 3b

Now let's look at two horizontal, four-note-per-string shapes that ascend the neck in a crawling pattern. These patterns are great for quickly covering a wide range of the fretboard and can produce some dynamic results when soloing.

Here is the shape that begins in third position. Notice that it has the same pattern of notes on *every string*, which makes it much easier to memorize.

Shape 3

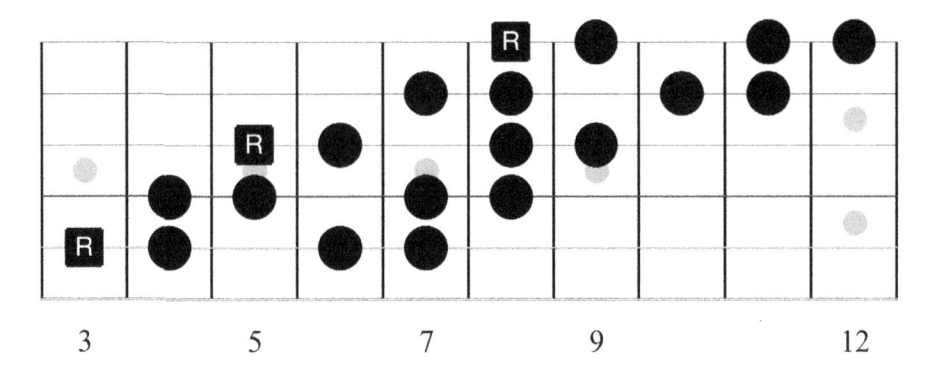

Example 3c

If you find it a stretch to play four notes on one string, especially in the lower register, then you can add a position slide, which is how I always play this pattern. Play the first note on the A string with your index finger, then immediately slide up one fret to play 4th fret also with the index finger. The remaining two notes are played with the ring and pinkie fingers respectively.

Execute the index finger slide on *every* string. When you've practiced this several times and are comfortable with the slide, you'll find that it facilitates playing the scale at speed.

Next, we'll play the crawling scale shape beginning on the low E string. Again, begin with the index finger and slide it up to play the next note. Each string has an identical four-note-per-string pattern as before.

When descending the scale, do the slide in reverse: play the highest note with the pinkie, the next note with the ring finger, the next with the index finger, then slide down one fret to play the final note of the pattern with the index finger.

Shape 4

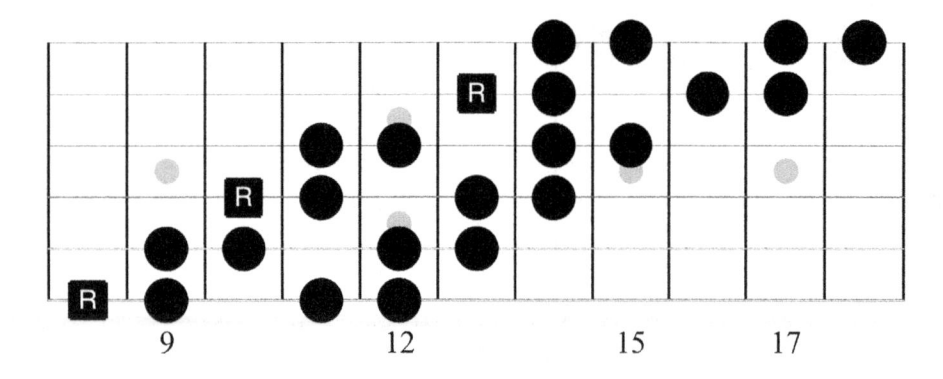

Example 3d

Spend a good amount of time practicing all four shapes ascending and descending until you begin to lock the patterns into muscle memory. If you're able, loop a static C7b9 chord to play over. It's important to internalize the *sound* of the scale and not just the shape.

Embedding the sound of the intervals

Now, let's look at some Diminished scale intervallic exercises similar to the ones in previous chapters. If you work carefully through each of these, you'll quickly internalize the intervals of the Diminished scale and be ready to put them to work in a creative context.

First, play through the scale ascending and descending in 3rds. Because of the unique construction of this scale, you'll hear that it never sounds like it resolves.

Example 3e

Let's try that again, but this time played with the up-down pattern.

Example 3f

I won't spell out everything for you here, but at the beginning of the chapter we explored several shapes we can use for the Diminished scale, and you can apply these intervallic patterns to each of them. Go back and work with all of the shapes, playing them in 3rds, then in 3rds up and down.

Example 3g shows the Diminished scale played in 4ths ascending. The fingering is exactly the same descending, so work out how to play it in reverse.

Example 3g

Now try playing the scale in 4ths with the up-down pattern. Here it is ascending and descending.

Example 3h

Playing the scale in 4ths as double-stops creates some cool sounding shapes you can use to create riff-like licks. On the audio, you'll hear this played ascending and descending.

Example 3i

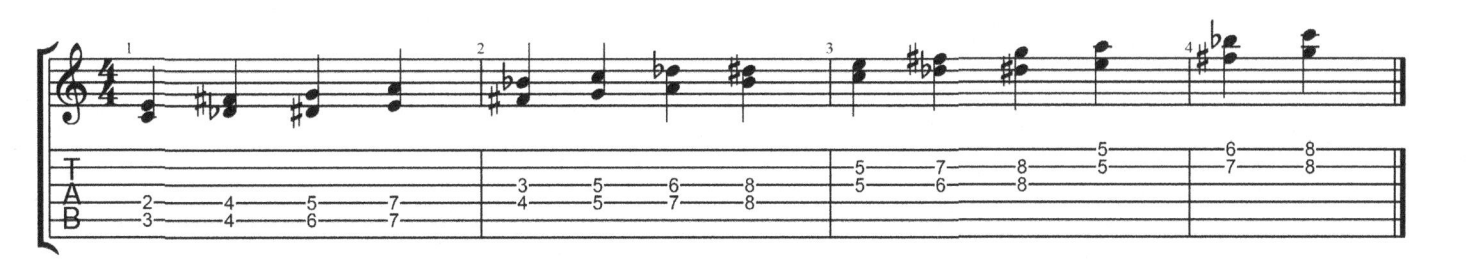

Now we'll play the Diminished scale in 5ths. This is an interesting exercise and you should recognize the pattern of how the intervals fall on the fretboard as tritones (flat 5ths). This way of playing the scale really highlights its dark, unresolved sound. Check it out!

55

Example 3j

Now play the scale in 5ths with the up-down pattern.

56

Example 3k

Now we're going to skip ahead to play the scale in 6ths.

Example 3l

Here, the scale is played in 6ths with the up-down pattern.

Example 3m

Finally, play through the scale with 6th intervals arranged as double-stops. It's worth experimenting with this sound for a while over a C7b9 vamp, as it's easy to create some distinctive sounding riff ideas. You can use this chapter's backing track to test it out.

Example 3n

Transposing the scale to other keys

The three-note-per-string patterns you learnt at the beginning of this chapter provide an easy way to transpose the Diminished scale to other keys. The musical examples that follow are based on a Bb dominant funk vamp, so we need to convert the scale from a C to a Bb tonal center.

Here's a reminder of the rule to create the diminished sound over a dominant chord:

Play the diminished scale a half step above the root of the dominant chord.

Over the Bb7 chord we'll therefore use the B Diminished scale. However, as before, we want to think of this scale from the *root of the chord* – so even though we are playing the B Diminished Scale, we are *anchoring* it on the Bb note, which is our tonal center.

To convert the scale shapes, you just need to shift them all down a tone from C to Bb. For Shape 3, for example, you'll now begin the pattern on the first fret of the A string.

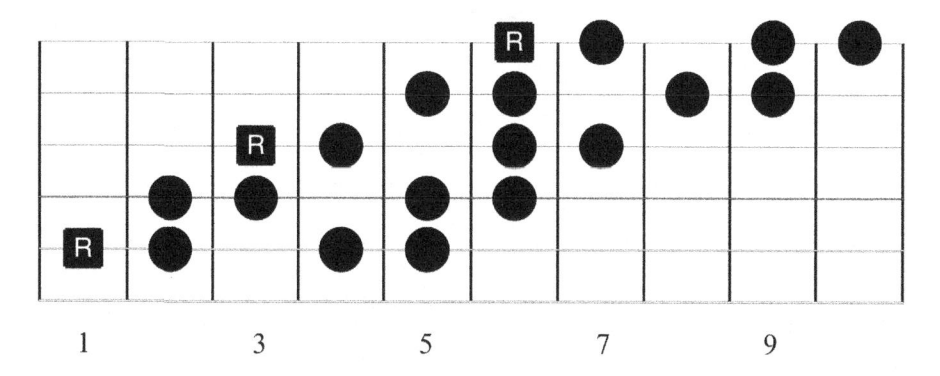

Revisit all of the scale shapes now and practice them with a Bb tonal center. Try some of the intervallic exercises too – don't just run up and down the scale shapes!

Building Diminished vocabulary

Now let's learn some diminished vocabulary. As before, we'll mix things up with some rock-blues licks. The lick that spans the first two bars creates a bluesy-diminished sound. The trick to achieving this effect is to play the blues scale but remove the 4th (in this case, a Bb blues scale minus the Eb note). The result is a scale shape that only uses notes found in the Diminished scale. The lick ends on an A note, rather than Ab, for added tension.

In bars 3-4, we move into a phrase that has wider intervals. If we break this idea down into its component parts, we see that it is two sets of 3rd intervals (beginning with the Db note on the 14th fret), followed by three sets of 5ths. The phrase crosses the bar line to end on a Db note in bar four to emphasize the b9 tension.

That's a lot of information to take in! It highlights the mercurial nature of the Diminished scale. First, take some time to absorb the *sound* of the phrase. You can probably hear that it wants to resolve to the Bb tonal center, but never quite arrives home. The resolution to this idea comes at the beginning of Example 3p.

Example 3o

The next line is a question and answer idea. The phrase in the pickup bar resolves the previous example and begins a bluesy "question" phrase. The "answer" begins at the end of bar one. It uses an identical rhythm but with Bb Half-Whole scale notes.

Playing an inside-sounding phrase, followed by an outside-sounding phrase with the same rhythm is a great way of introducing tension into your playing. Your audience will latch onto the strong rhythm and more readily accept the outside sound because they have a frame of reference for it.

Example 3p

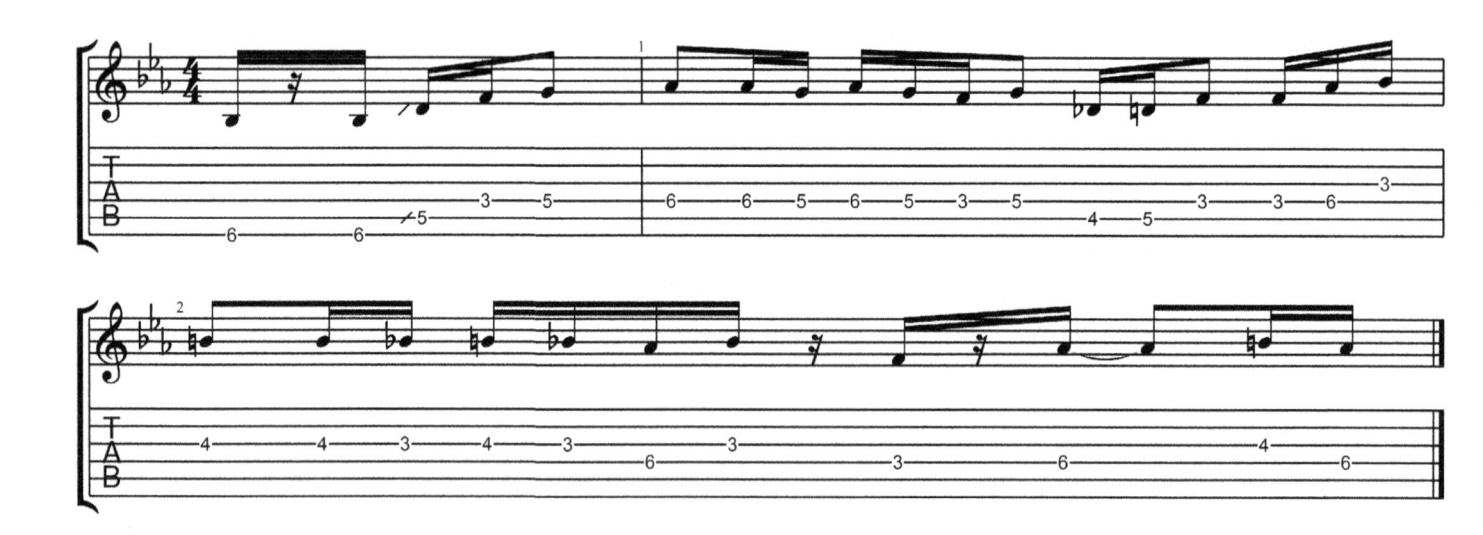

In bar one of Example 3q, the line uses Bb Half-Whole scale notes until the last three-note phrase. The C, A and E notes played here, when superimposed over the Bb7 vamp, imply a Bb13(#11) chord, which creates a Bb Lydian Dominant type sound. Sometimes I forget about the scale and just focus on targeting notes that will create a specific tension over the harmony.

Example 3q

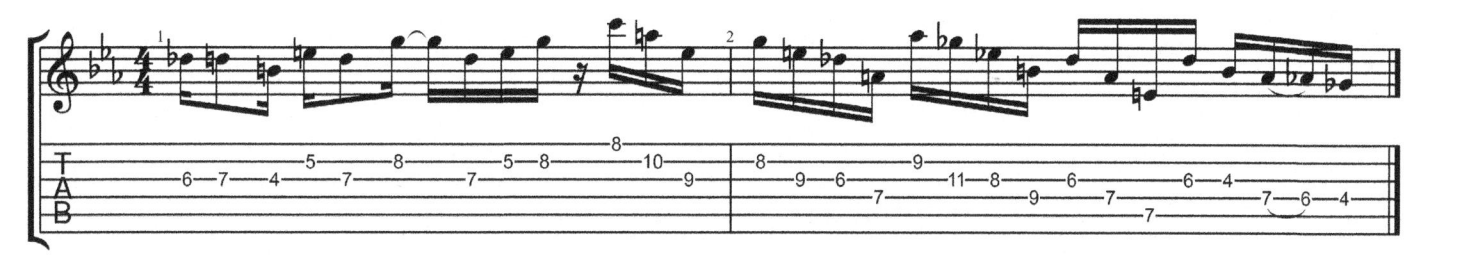

The next idea begins in major blues territory but gradually morphs into a Diminished scale line. The familiar inside-sounding line lays the foundation for the tension that will follow. The main challenge here is to nail the feel of the cascading run in bars 3-4. Listen to the audio and study how I play it.

Example 3r

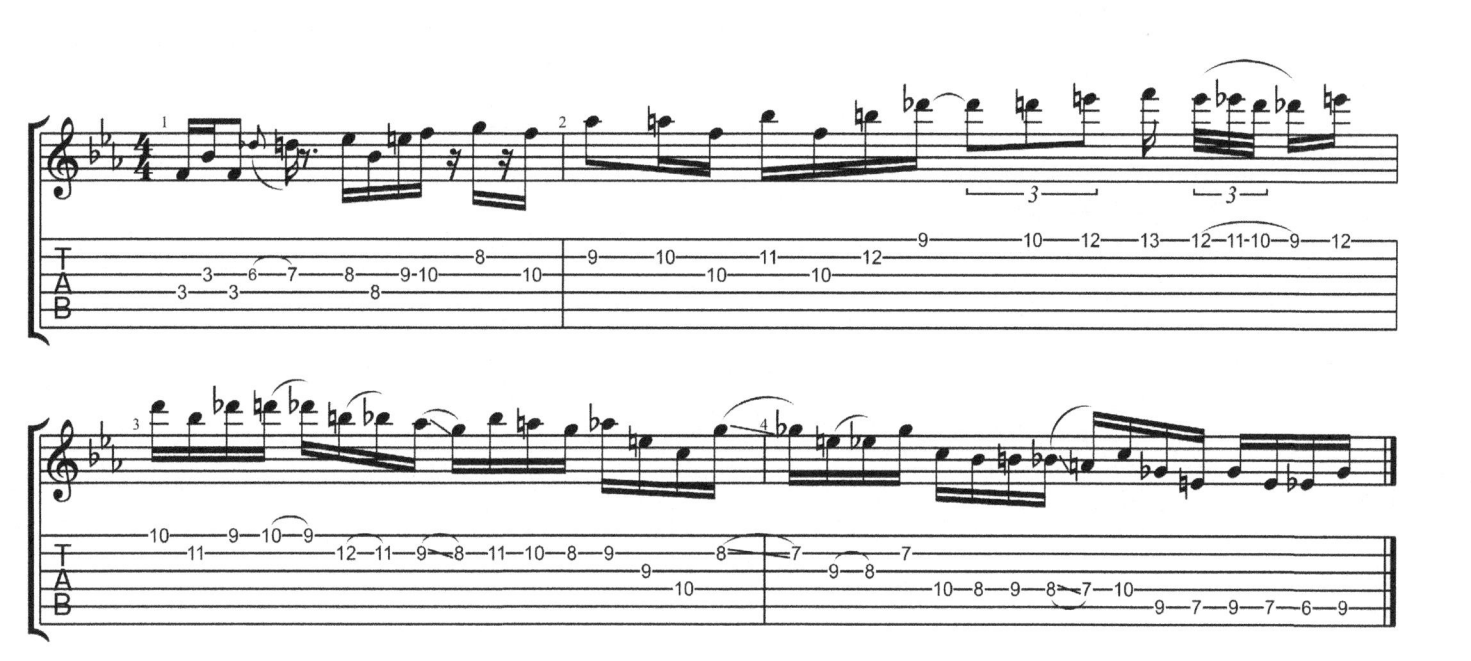

Here's a challenging lick for you to work on. After the opening blues bends there is a long, mostly 1/32nd note passage that spans bars 3-4. The only way to approach a line like this is to slow things right down and learn it in smaller sections. In bar three, after the triplet phrase, you should learn the line as two groups of eight notes. In bar four, break the line into four groups of notes before bringing them together.

Once you are comfortable with all the component parts, connect them together (still playing slowly), before gradually bringing the lick up to speed.

Example 3s

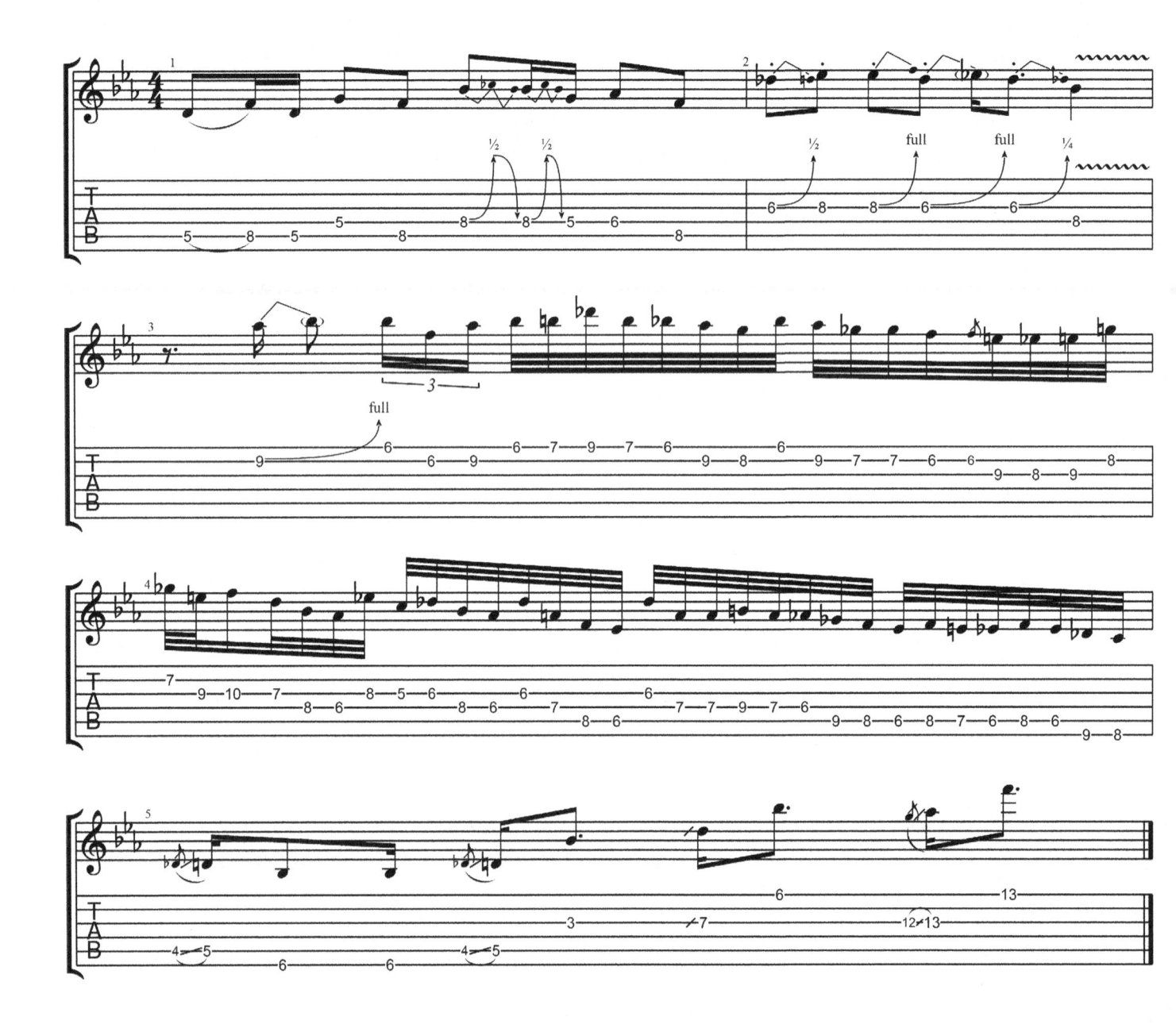

The next example features a repeating sequence idea. Listen to the audio and you'll hear it immediately. After the opening blues-influenced phrase we have four groups of four-note phrases – in each case a 1/32 note triplet followed by a 1/16th note – each spelling the diminished sound.

In the second half of bar two there is a chromatic-infused diminished run up to a target note of B (A string, fret 14), after which the sequencing idea begins again. This time I develop the idea into five-note phrases.

Example 3t

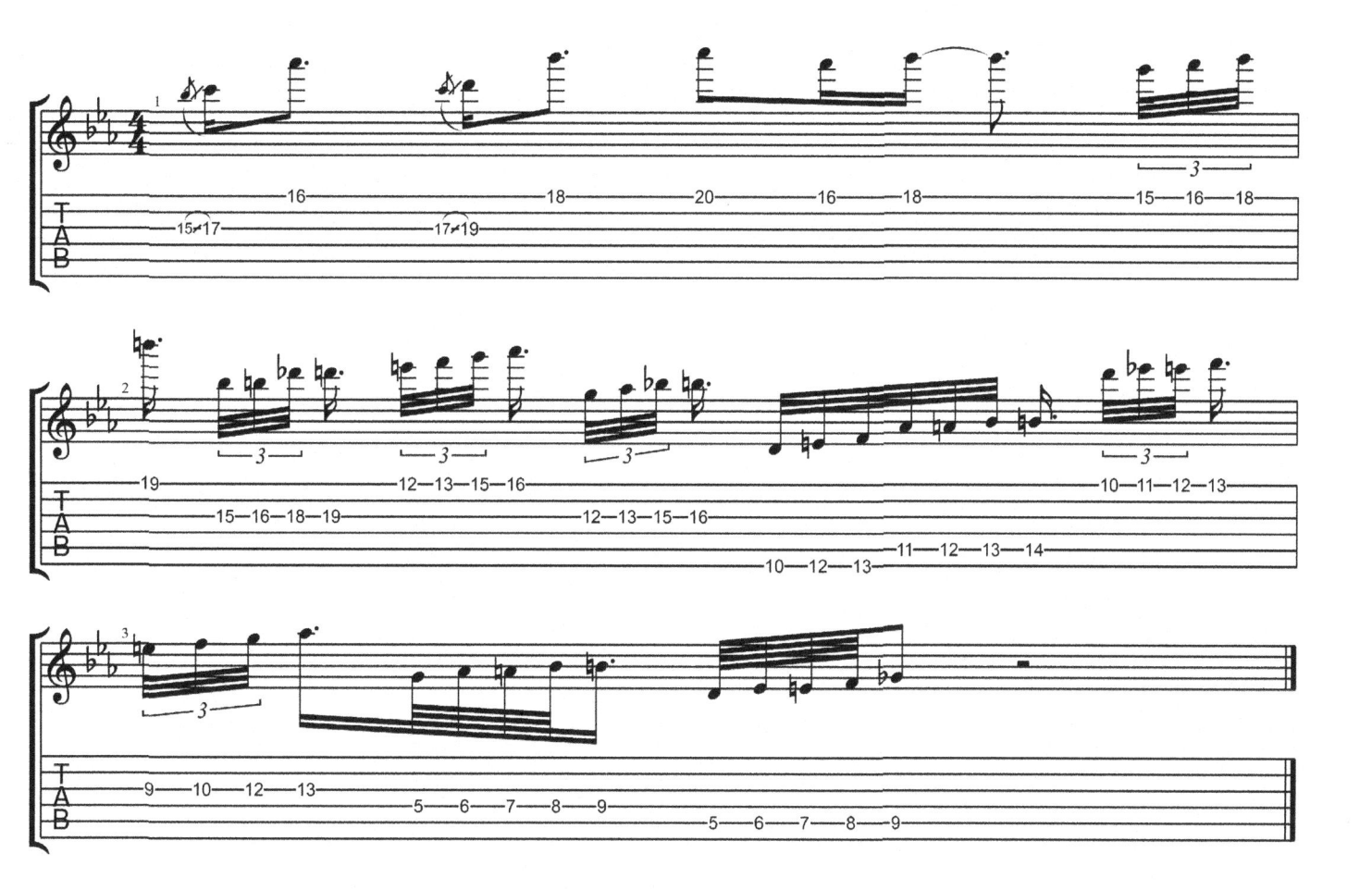

Here is a line that begins outside, goes inside, then gradually moves outside again. Although the whole line is organized into groups of short four-note phrases, it has a heavy 1/16th note triplet feel that pulls against the funk groove underneath. Listen carefully to the audio and play along with me to capture the timing and feel. It's important to make it groove.

In bar four, this part of the lick exploits the symmetry of the Diminished scale. Remember that diminished phrases can be moved around the fretboard in minor 3rds (three frets), so you can move any diminished lick or sequence up or down the neck in three-fret increments.

Example 3u

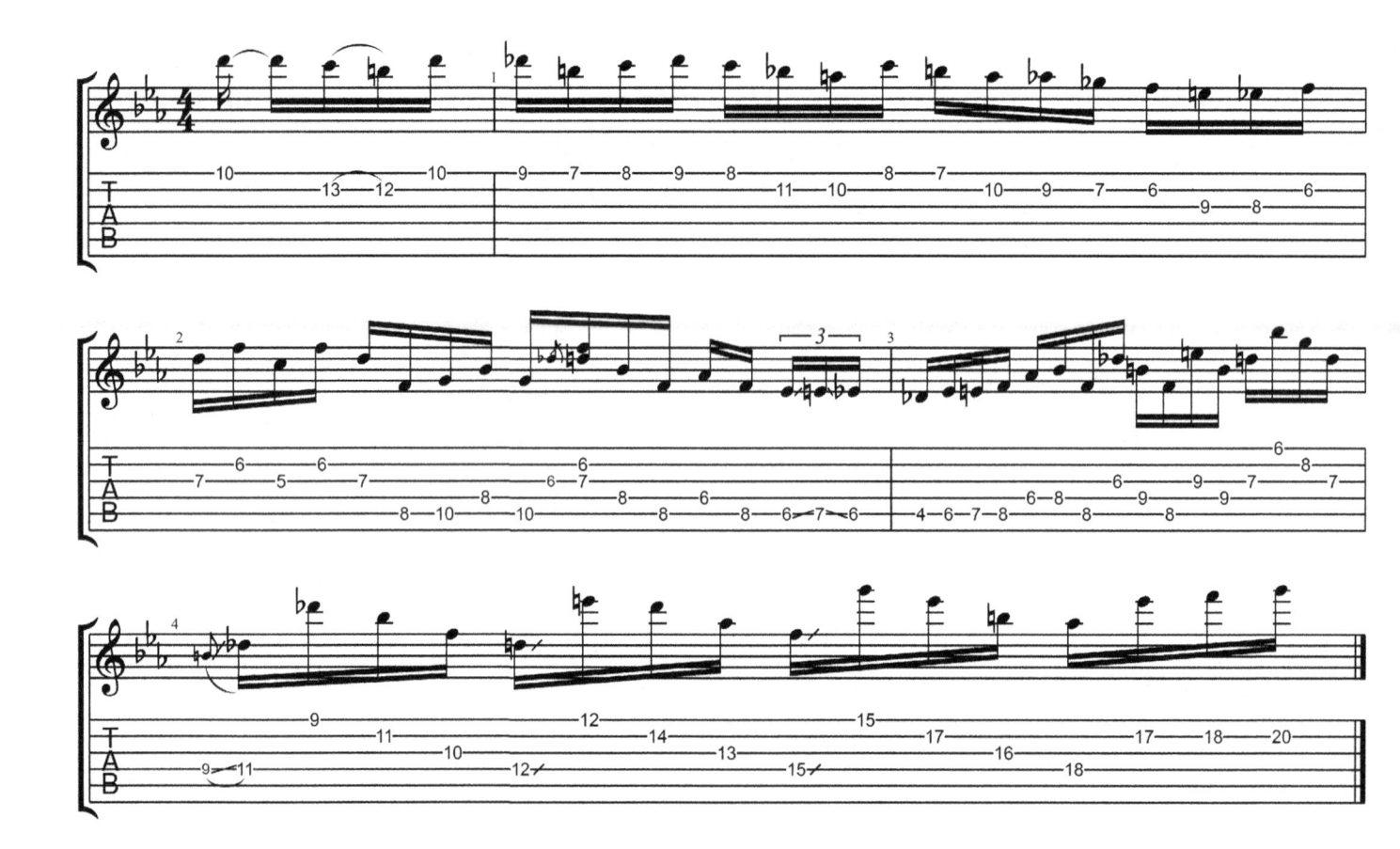

The focal point of the next example is in bars 3-4. Again, I am thinking about what tensions from Bb Half-Whole can be superimposed over the underlying Bb7 harmony. Each short phrase contains tension notes that suggest the sound of Bb7alt, rather than a straight Bb7 chord.

Example 3v

Next is a lick that begins with an ascending line which carries over into the beginning of bar two. While it mostly comprises Bb Half-Whole scale notes, I have added some passing tones to create a smoother line.

For the rest of this lick, I bring back the sequencing idea seen earlier, but this time there are larger string skips between the phrases. Bar three relies on the symmetrical pattern of the scale and the way it lends itself to ideas that move in minor thirds. Conveniently, if we play an idea on the G string, it can be repeated, fret-for-fret, on the high (or low) E string, and the result will be two phrases a minor 3rd apart.

Example 3w

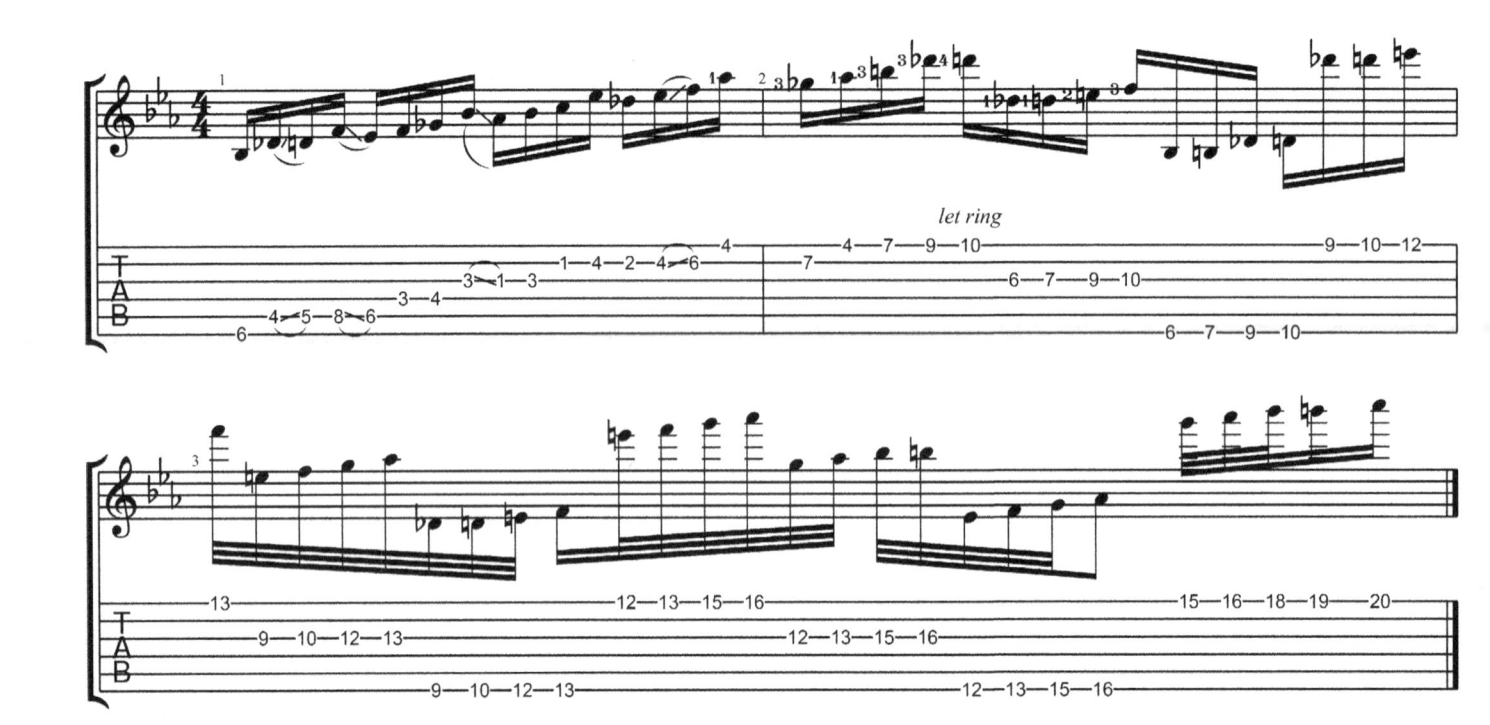

Example 3x completes the sequencing idea of the previous example. The string skipping idea that begins in the first half of bar one almost disguises the standard blues lick that fills the first half of bar two, then the altered sound continues.

Example 3x

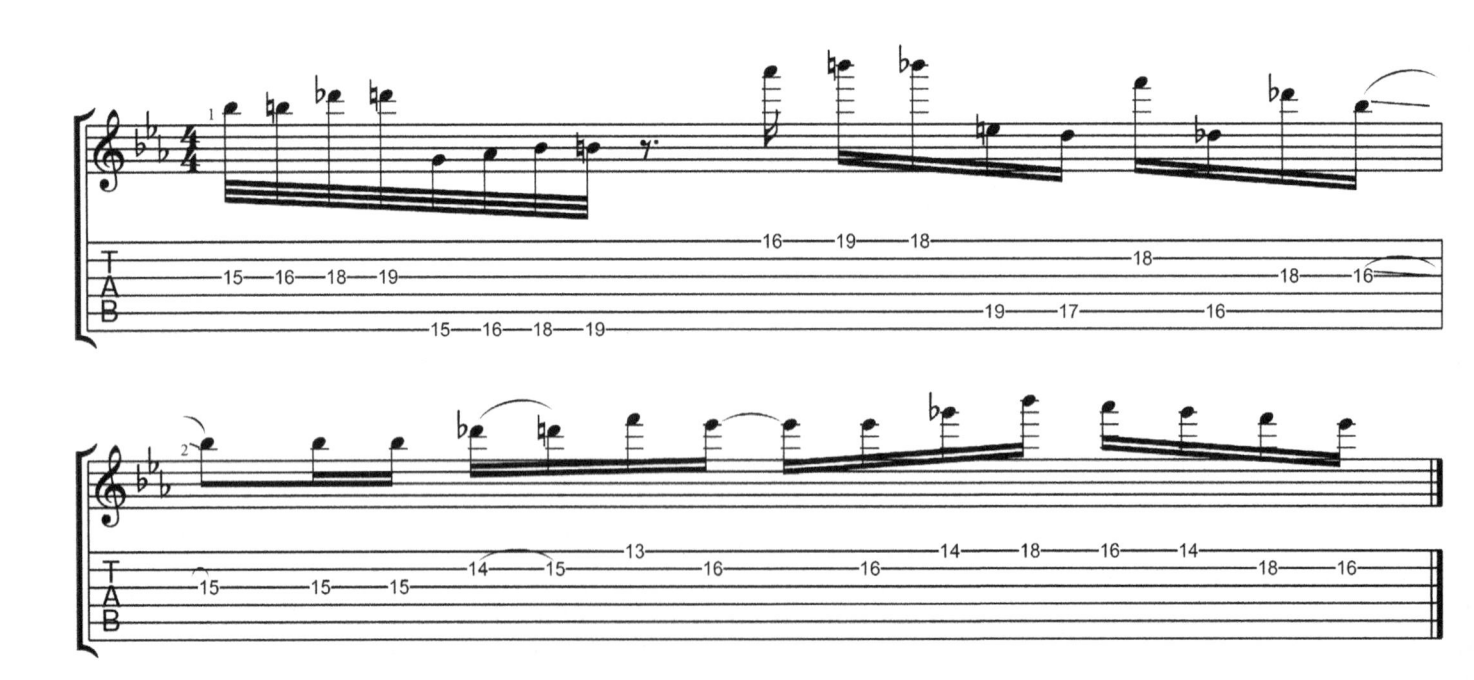

Finally, here is a cascading descending line, the ultimate goal of which is to land on the Bb in bar four to ground the harmony.

Example 3y

After practicing the individual lines and phrases above, it's time to tackle the full solo. A few of the phrases will fall in slightly different places in the bar. Listen to the solo all the way through, then break it down and approach it one phrase at a time. You'll hear where I take breaths in the solo – i.e. where one idea ends and another begins. Work on isolating and nailing the individual runs and motifs.

Example 3z

69

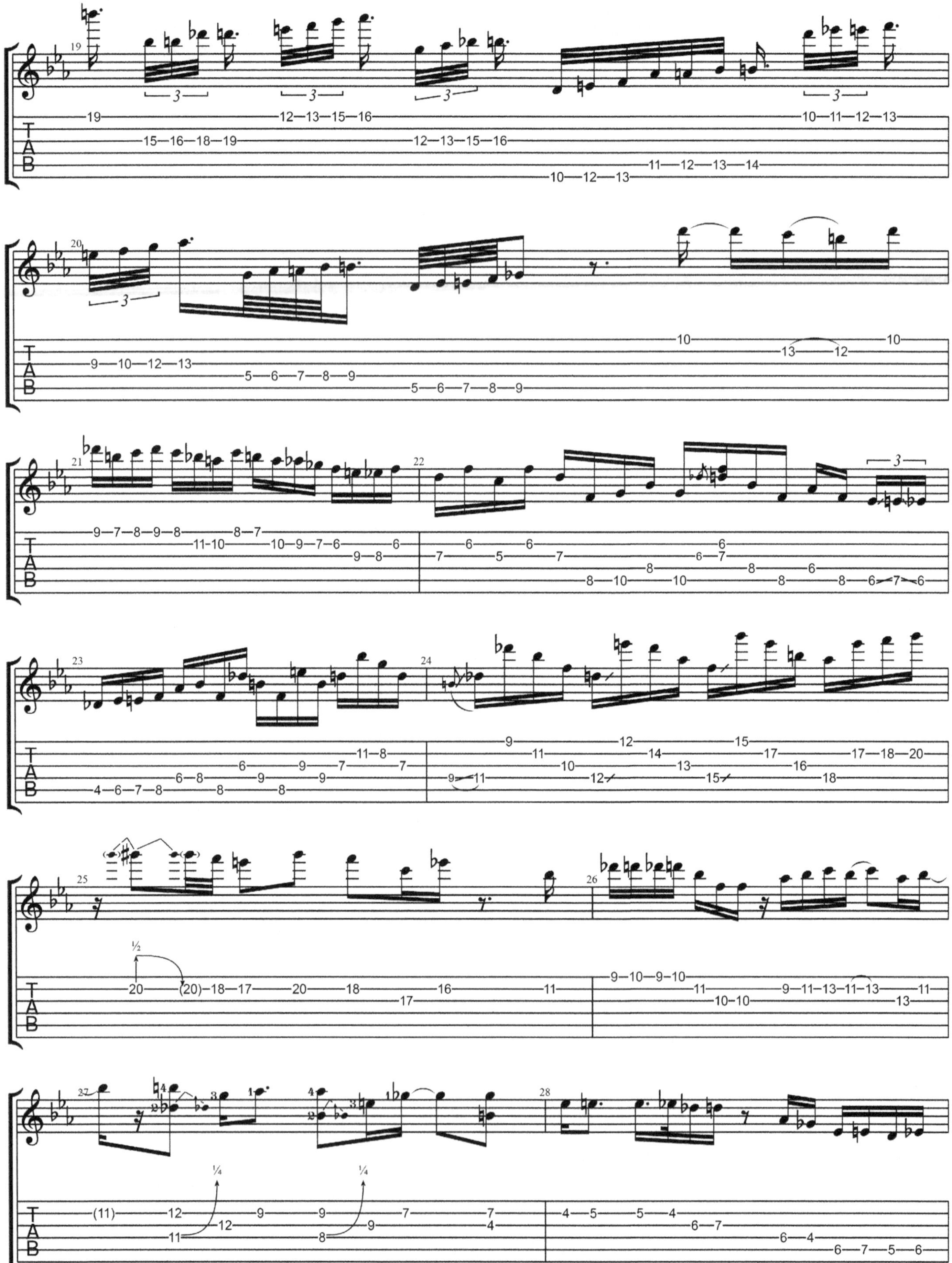

71

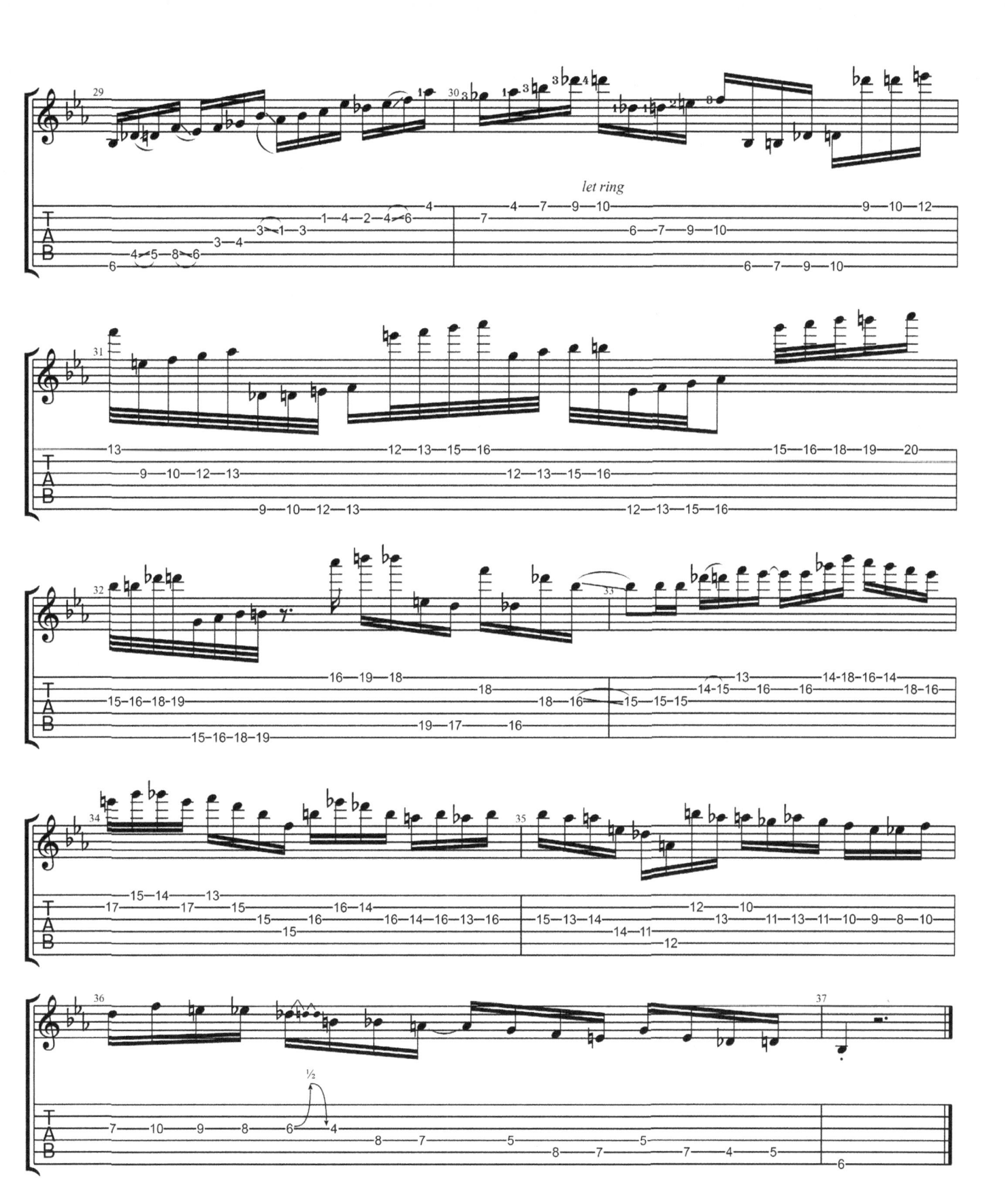

Chapter Four – The Altered Scale

The Altered scale originates from the Melodic Minor scale. Also known as the Super Locrian, it is the seventh mode of the Melodic Minor and contains all the altered tensions that can be added to a dominant chord.

Below are the notes of the C Altered scale and the intervals it highlights when played over a C7 chord (C E G Bb):

C Altered

C	Db	D#	E	Gb	G#	Bb
Root	b9	#9	3rd	b5	#5	b7

C Altered contains the root, 3rd and b7 of C7, plus every possible alteration that can be made to a dominant chord, giving us b5, #5, b9 and #9 tension notes.

This makes the scale the perfect choice for easy access to some vivid color tensions over dominant chords. We can choose to target specific tension notes within the scale, such as just the b9 sound, or just use all the available tensions to create more complex inside-outside melodic lines.

With that small amount of theory out of the way, let me tell you how I view this scale and how I apply it in real musical situations.

To me, the Altered scale is a combination of the Diminished and Whole Tone scales and understanding this makes it much easier to learn. Here is how I visualize it on the fretboard. Take a look at this third position, A string root scale shape:

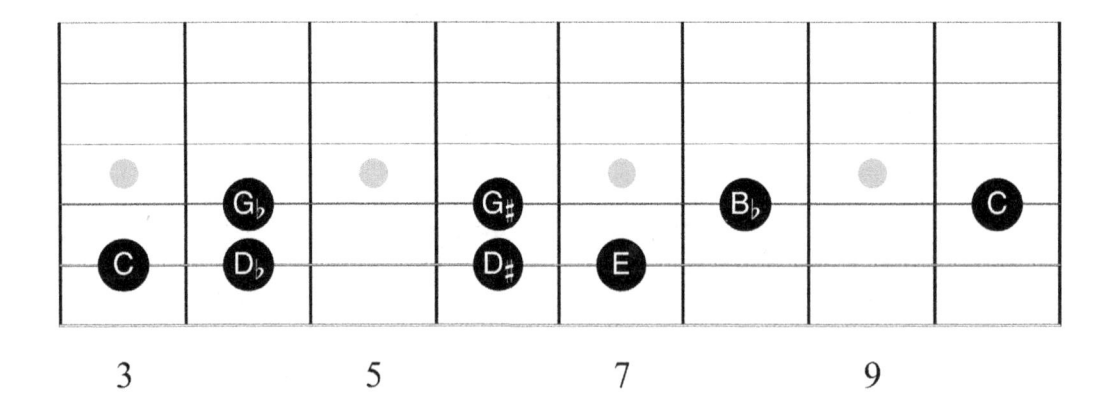

Notice that the four notes on the A string mirror those of the Diminished scale (highlighted in bold type):

C# Diminished = **C, Db, D#, E,** F#, G, A, Bb

While the four notes on the D string mirror those of the Whole Tone scale.

C Whole Tone = C, D, E, **Gb, Ab/G#, Bb,** C

The C root note connects these two scale fragments together.

The above pattern repeats across string sets and we can simply repeat it to ascend/descend the neck rapidly, covering most of the fretboard.

When I use the Altered scale to create melodic ideas, I visualize this pattern on the fretboard – a Diminished pattern on one string and a Whole Tone pattern on the next.

In practice, this means I can easily play a mixture of Diminished and Whole Tone ideas by focusing on the different sides of the scale. I know that the Diminished side contains the b9 and #9 tension notes, and the Whole Tone side has the b5 and #5. Lots of the contemporary vocabulary I use comes out of exploiting this geometric pattern for the scale.

We can play the sequence a little more economically by relocating a note from the Whole Tone segment of the scale onto the next string, like this:

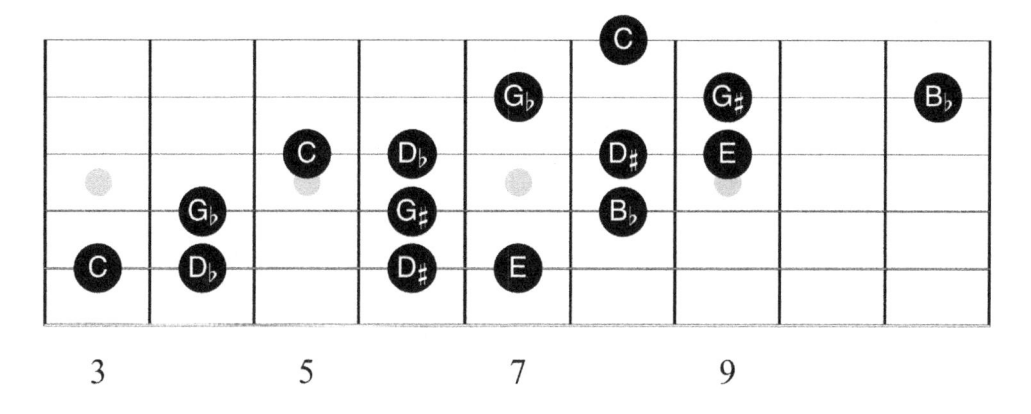

Play the scale ascending, beginning on the A string, third fret. When descending, you can add in the scale notes that occur on the low E string but remember that it's important to be able to visualize and know the scale shape from its root.

Example 4a

Next, play through the scale shape with the root note on the low E string, eighth fret. Listen to how it sounds over a C7#5 chord.

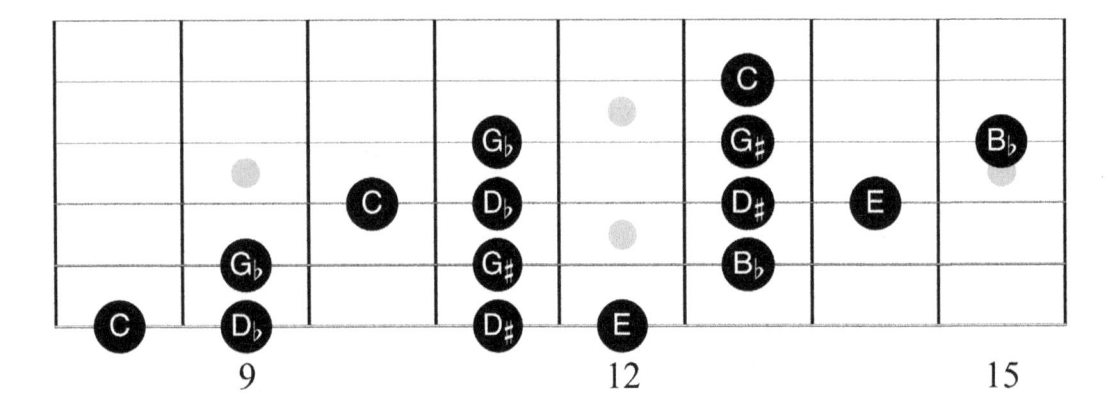

We can, of course, extend this pattern further up the fretboard, as you'll hear in Example 4b.

Example 4b

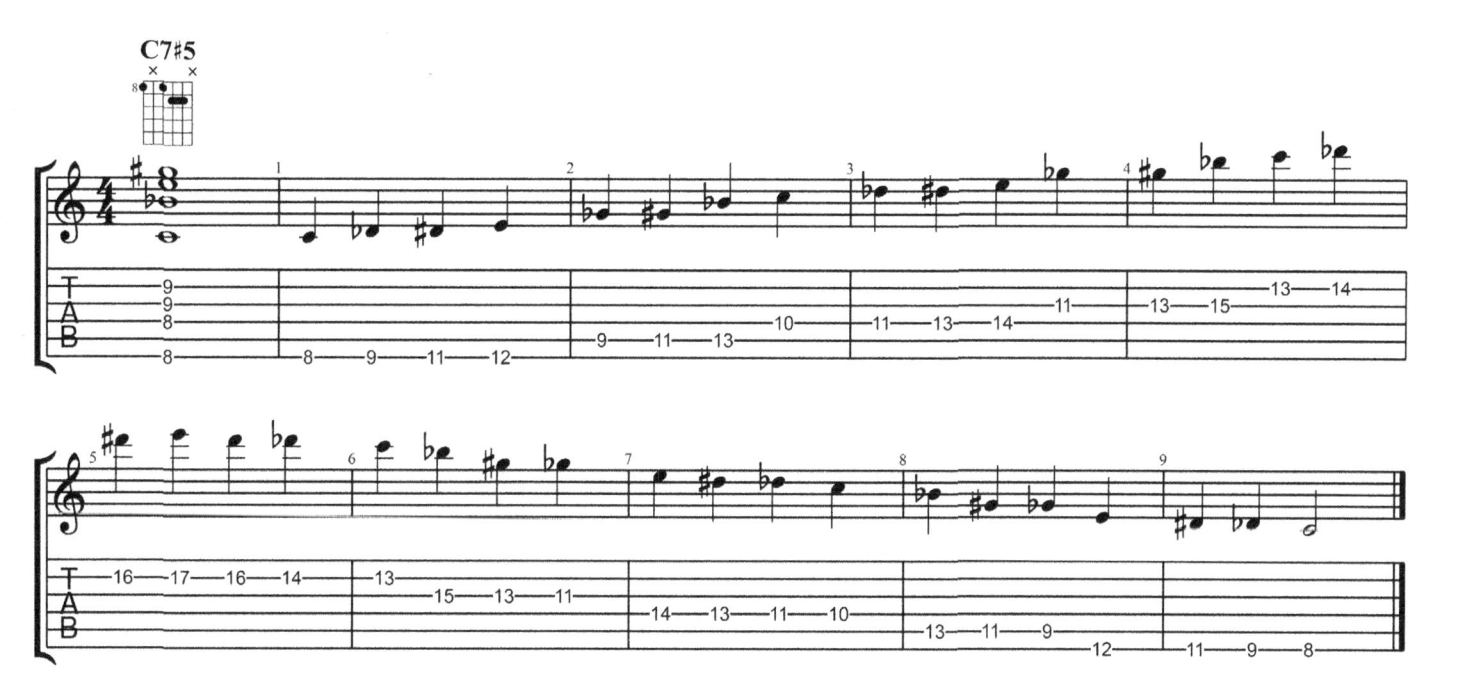

Practice these scale shapes until the sound of the intervals begin to sound as natural and predictable to you as the major scale.

Embedding the sound of the intervals

Following the method we've used throughout this book, we'll now work through some of the Altered scale's intervals in order to further embed its sound.

We'll begin by playing the C Altered scale arranged in 3rds, ascending and descending.

Example 4c

Now try it with the up-down pattern and play over a looped C7b9 chord.

How does the scale sound to you? How would you describe its color, compared to the Diminished scale in the previous chapter? To my ears, the Altered scale sounds more stable than the Diminished scale, but it still has plenty of tension.

Example 4d

You can always play intervals simultaneously to form double-stop type shapes. These can be useful when comping or to create riff-like solos. Here we have double-stops based on 3rds.

Example 4e

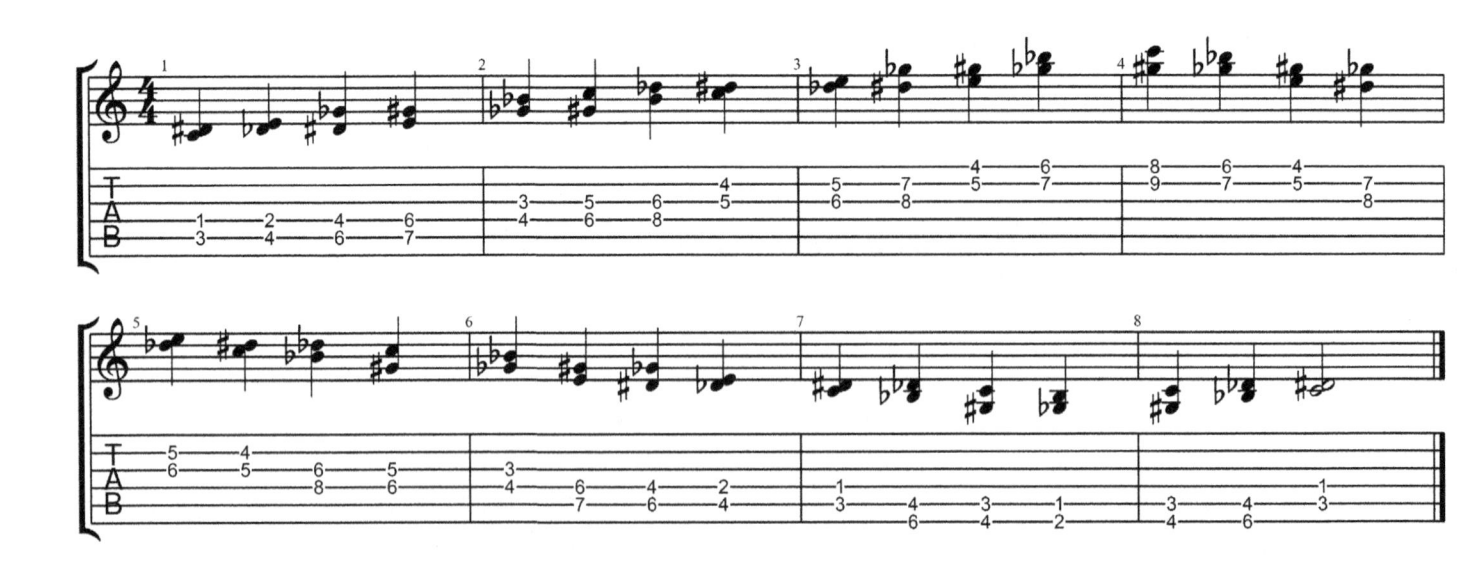

Next, let's hear the scale played in 4ths. We'll skip straight to playing it with the up-down pattern.

76

Example 4f

Now let's apply the up-down pattern again, but this time with 5th intervals.

Example 4g

Playing 6ths with the Altered scale obviously produces a different effect to the country-style effect of the Major scale, but they sound great over altered dominant chords and are easy to play. For practice, work out the up-down pattern for C Altered in 6ths, and also try these shapes as double-stops.

Example 4h

The final four exercises explore the Altered scale in wider intervals – 7ths and 9ths. As the distance between the intervals increases, it becomes more important to get the fretting hand into position a split second before you need to play the next phrase, as some jumping around the fretboard is required.

Everyone will have their preferences when it comes to fingering these intervals, so all I'll say is, *plan ahead* and aim to shift position in a logical manner. If you find a different way of playing the exercise than is written below, do feel free to change it!

Here is C Altered organized in 7ths.

Example 4i

Now play through the scale in 7ths using the up-down pattern. You'll hear that these wider intervals almost take on the sound of a classical etude.

Example 4j

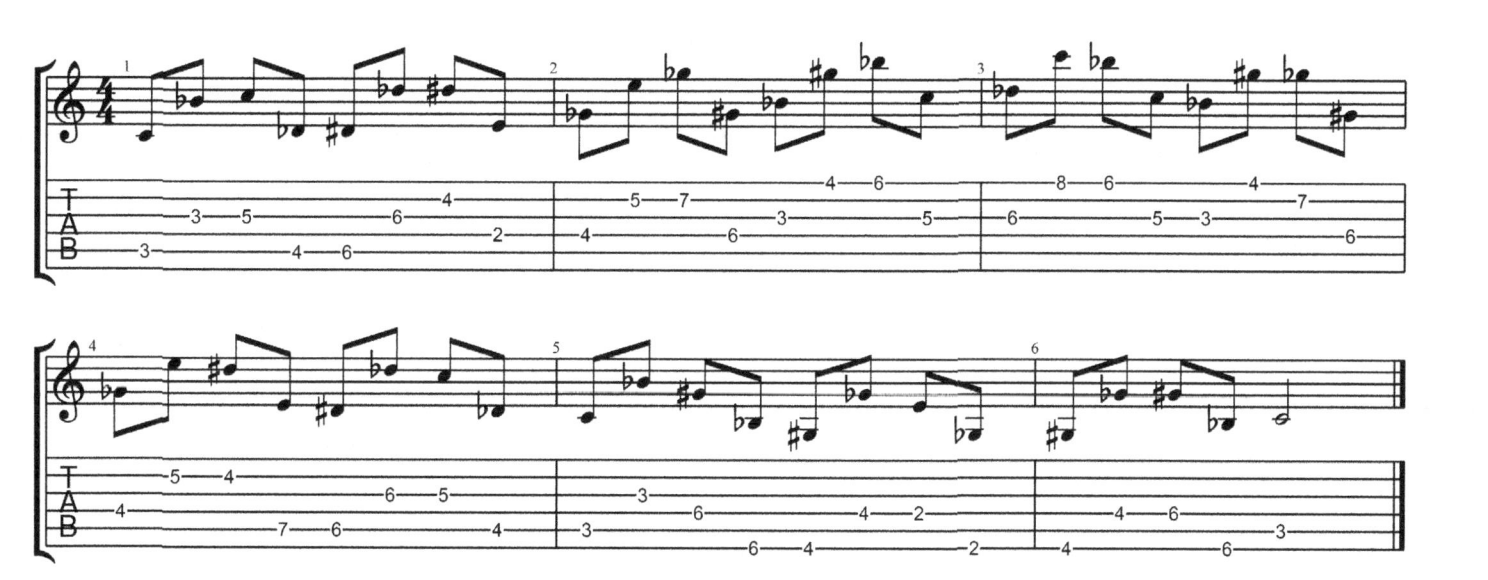

Finally, we'll play through the scale in 9ths. First straight, then with the up-down pattern. These exercises contain large skips, so make sure you play them cleanly.

Example 4k

Focus on your fretting hand positioning for this exercise and make alterations if you find a way of playing it that better suits your technique.

Example 41

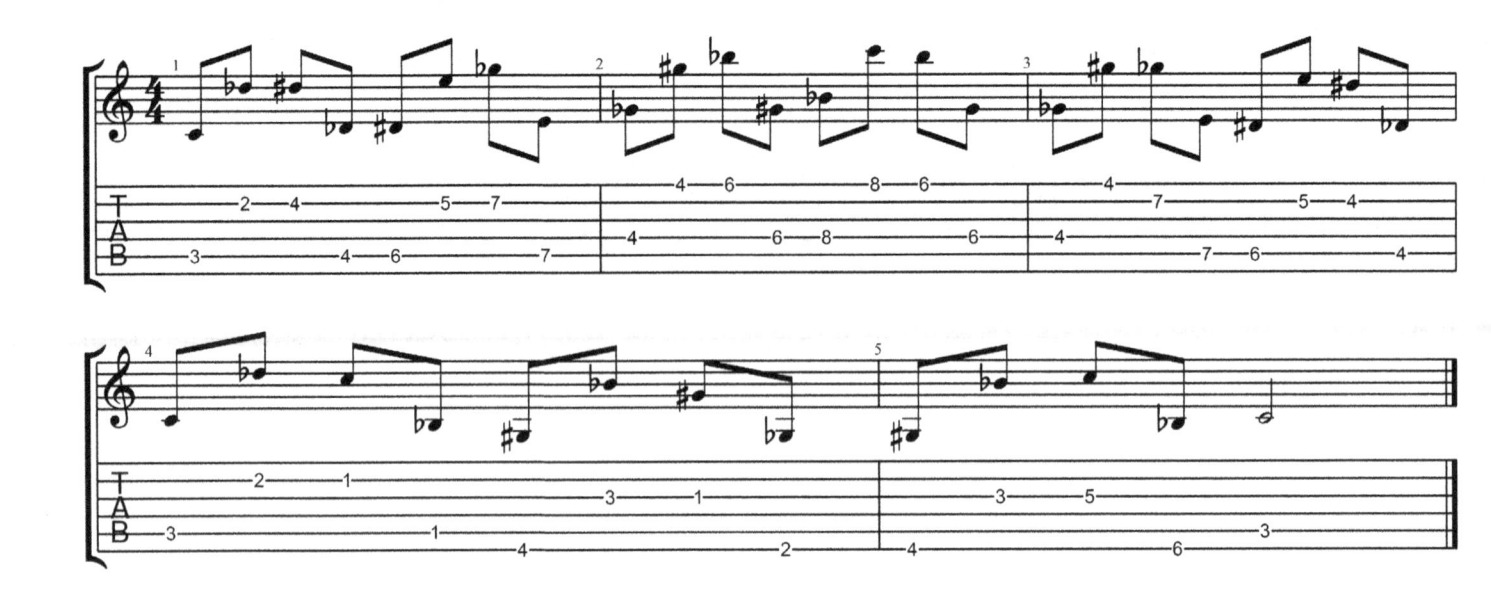

Converting the scale to other keys

Now we can move onto tackling some melodic lines. The following Altered scale vocabulary is played over a funky vamp on a D9 chord, which means we'll need to transpose the scale up a tone to play the D Altered scale.

I advise you to work through the interval exercises again, transposing them to D. It's important that you train your ears to really *hear* and internalize those intervals.

Use the scale shapes you learnt earlier and practice them over a D7#9 chord. Here's a diagram showing an economical fifth position shape for D Altered. Revise the low E string shape during your next practice session.

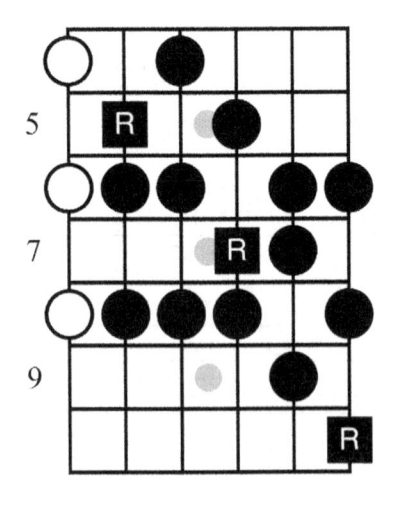

Adding triads and arpeggios

So far, we have only approached the Altered color via its scale patterns, but there are other rich-sounding structures contained within the scale that we can use to create melodic lines.

Before we get into the vocabulary, I want to quickly show you how you can build triads and arpeggios from any note of the altered scale. These structures are great ways to break up the scale patterns and introduce new soloing ideas.

If we harmonize the Altered scale in the traditional way (by stacking notes in 3rds), it produces two diminished triads, two minor triads, two major triads, and one augmented triad. Here are the notes of D Altered:

D	Eb	F	Gb	Ab	Bb	C

Beginning with the D root note, if we stack alternate notes to form a triad, we get D diminished (D, F, Ab). Moving to the second note, stacking 3rds produces Eb minor (Eb, Gb, Bb). Continuing this process, we end up with the following set of triads:

Ddim	Ebm	Fm	GbAug	AbMaj	BbMaj	Cdim
D F Ab	Eb Gb Bb	F Ab C	Gb Bb D	Ab C Eb	Bb D F	C Eb Gb

We can use these simple structures to build lines when soloing, but we can also add a fourth note to each of them to form 7th arpeggios structures.

Dm7b5	Ebm(Maj7)	Fm7	GbMaj7#5	Ab7	Bb7	Cm7b5
D F Ab C	Eb Gb Bb D	F Ab C Eb	Gb Bb D F	Ab C Eb Gb	Bb D F Ab	C Eb Gb Bb

Play through the following exercise that cycles through these arpeggios. Listen and absorb their sound. For practice, work out how to play them in a different area of the neck.

Example 4m

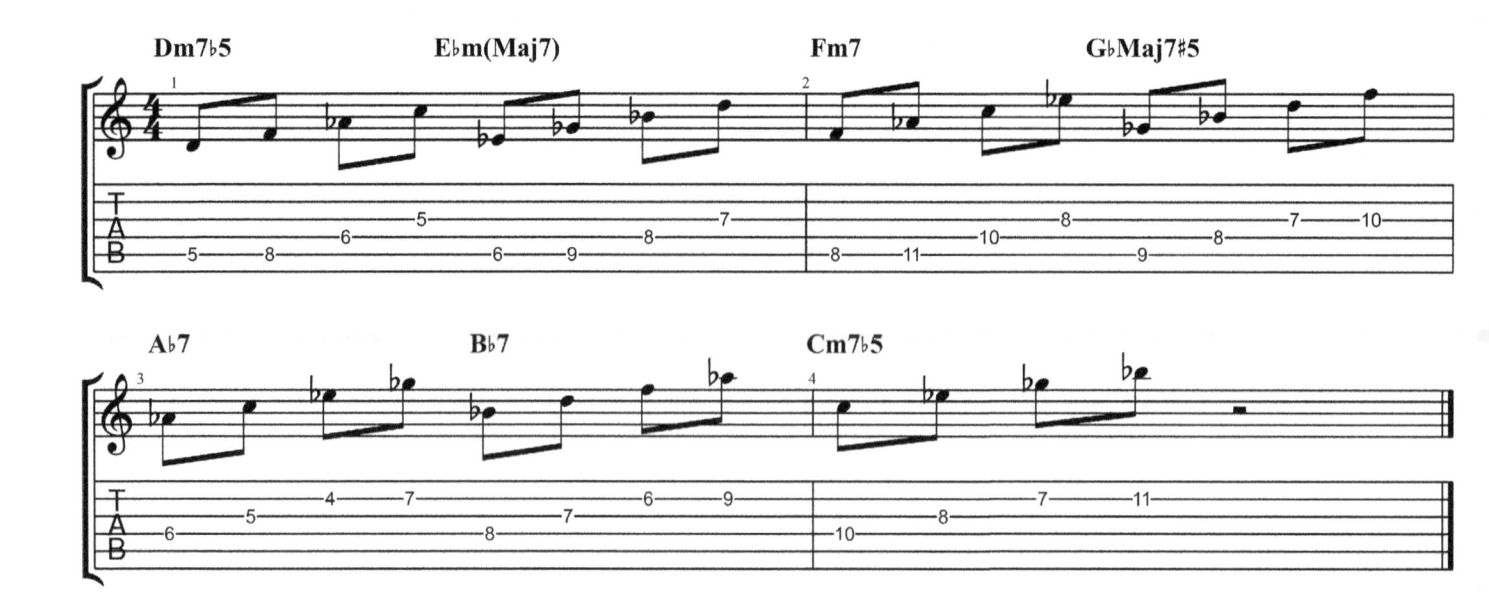

Although we are only scratching the surface here, you can see from the above table/exercise that exploring the arpeggios native to the D Altered scale can produce some interesting tonal colors. These arpeggios have the potential to generate melodic ideas you might not have thought to use over a D dominant vamp.

So, how can we explore this idea further?

There is always the danger of being overwhelmed with options when drilling down into a scale like this, and we can often just give up and revert to playing what we know, rather than breaking new ground. To avoid this, I suggest taking just *one* of the diatonic arpeggios above and improvising with it over a D7 vamp to hear the sound it creates.

For example, take the GbMaj7#5 arpeggio and use it to play over the D7 vamp backing track that accompanies this chapter.

The GbMaj7#5 arpeggio has the notes Gb, Bb, D and F.

The D and Gb (enharmonically named F#) notes can be found in the D Mixolydian scale, while the Bb and F notes are specific to the D Altered scale.

This means you have two *inside* sounding notes and two *outside* sounding notes to experiment with. Test out this idea now and see what simple licks and phrases you can create using *only* this arpeggio over the backing track.

To help you, I've included a diagram below that shows the arpeggio mapped across the fretboard. Spend some time exploring the notes and play any obvious geometric patterns that stand out to you to form short phrase. You should find that you'll quickly create some new vocabulary.

GbMaj7#5 Arpeggio Map

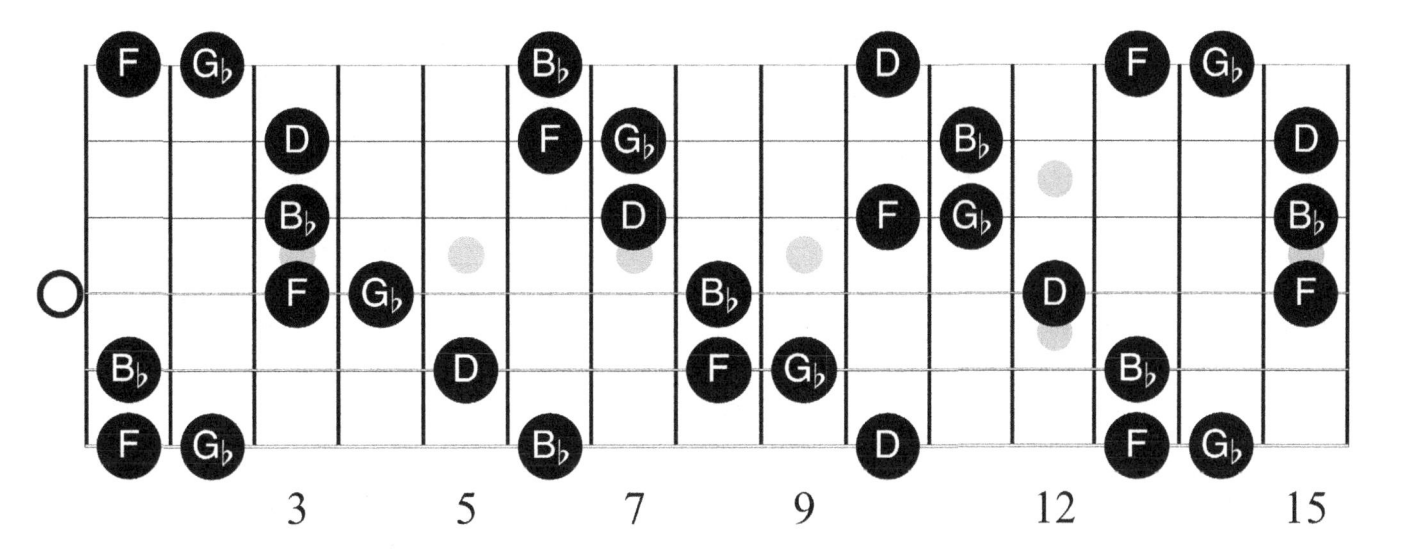

This is a creative way of building fresh sounding melodic ideas into your soloing. When you have exhausted your ideas using this arpeggio, go back to the table and pick a different one. Create your own fretboard map and use only the new arpeggio to generate more melodic phrases. It's a good way to build your vocabulary without suffering from information overload.

Building Altered scale vocabulary

Now let's look at how to apply the Altered scale in a soloing context.

When playing over the D7 vamp accompanying this chapter, I felt it was crying out for some Stevie Ray Vaughn type blues licks alongside the Altered scale runs and sequences. Often, the tempo and key of a piece will suggest different ideas and it's a matter of going with the flow and seeing where the music leads you. There are quite a few arpeggiated passages in the examples below, so your picking technique will need to be on-point to play them as cleanly as possible. If you choose to use an overdriven tone like me, make sure the gain isn't disguising poor technique!

NB: For ease of reading these ideas are shown in the key of G Major (viewing D7 as the V chord). This makes it much easier to spot when I play an altered note in the notation.

This first example starts and ends with a bluesy idea and subtly introduces Altered scale notes via the fast trills that begin in the second half of bar three. The line just hints at what is to come.

Example 4n

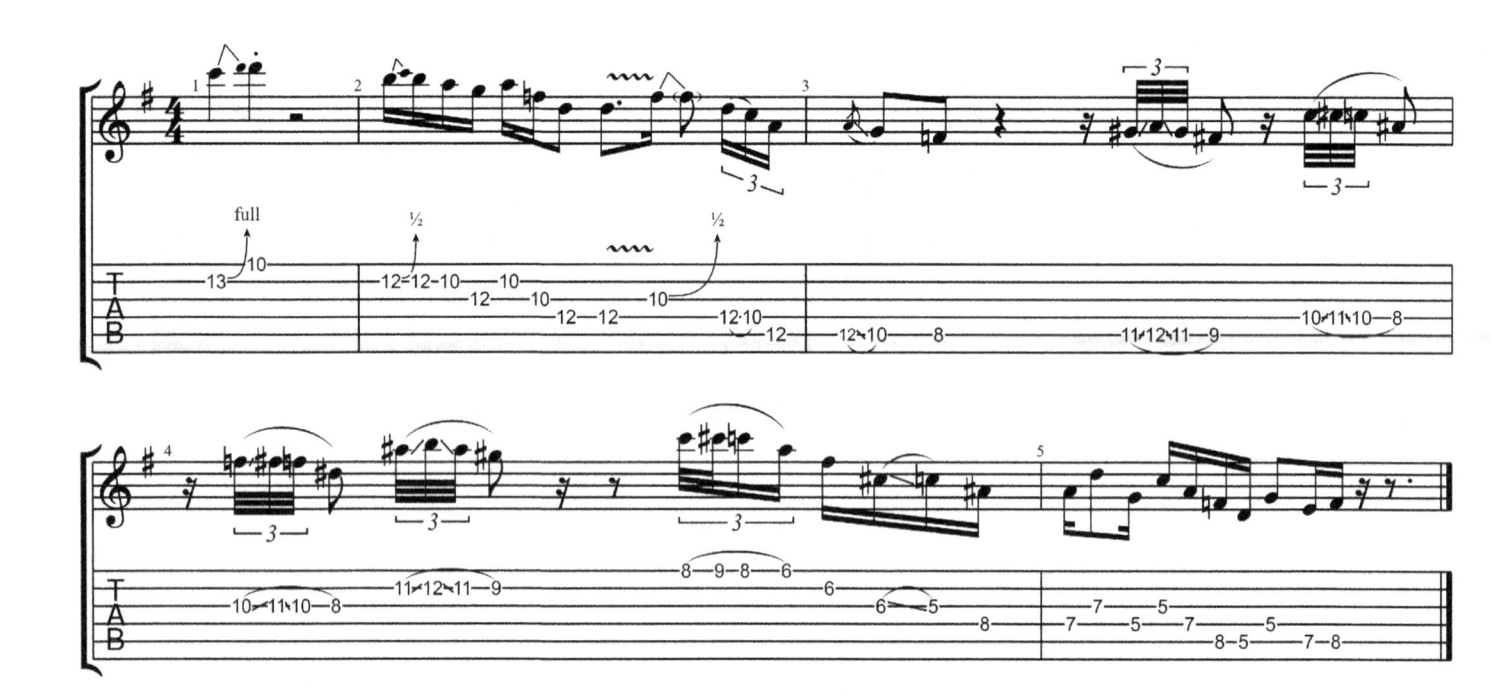

Here's an example of how I like to "disguise" a blues lick to change things up. Essentially, I'm playing a simple pentatonic idea, but the addition of chromatic passing notes creates more interest and movement.

Example 4o

After a brief blues lick at the beginning of bar one, this lick launches into an Altered scale arpeggio idea. The palm-muted ascending run in the second half of bar one begins with a variation of the Ebm(Maj7) arpeggio from the harmonized melodic minor scale we looked at earlier (I'm also adding the 9th). As the line descends, I sequence the arpeggio, changing the order of the notes. If you work with a fretboard map of the arpeggio, you'll be able to develop your own, similar ideas.

For the rest of the line, I use a pedal tone idea where I target a note in the scale and keep returning to it after playing nearby scale tones. It's not a pedal tone in the strictest sense, but my approach is essentially to target a specific zone on the neck and see what melodic ideas can be developed around it.

Example 4p

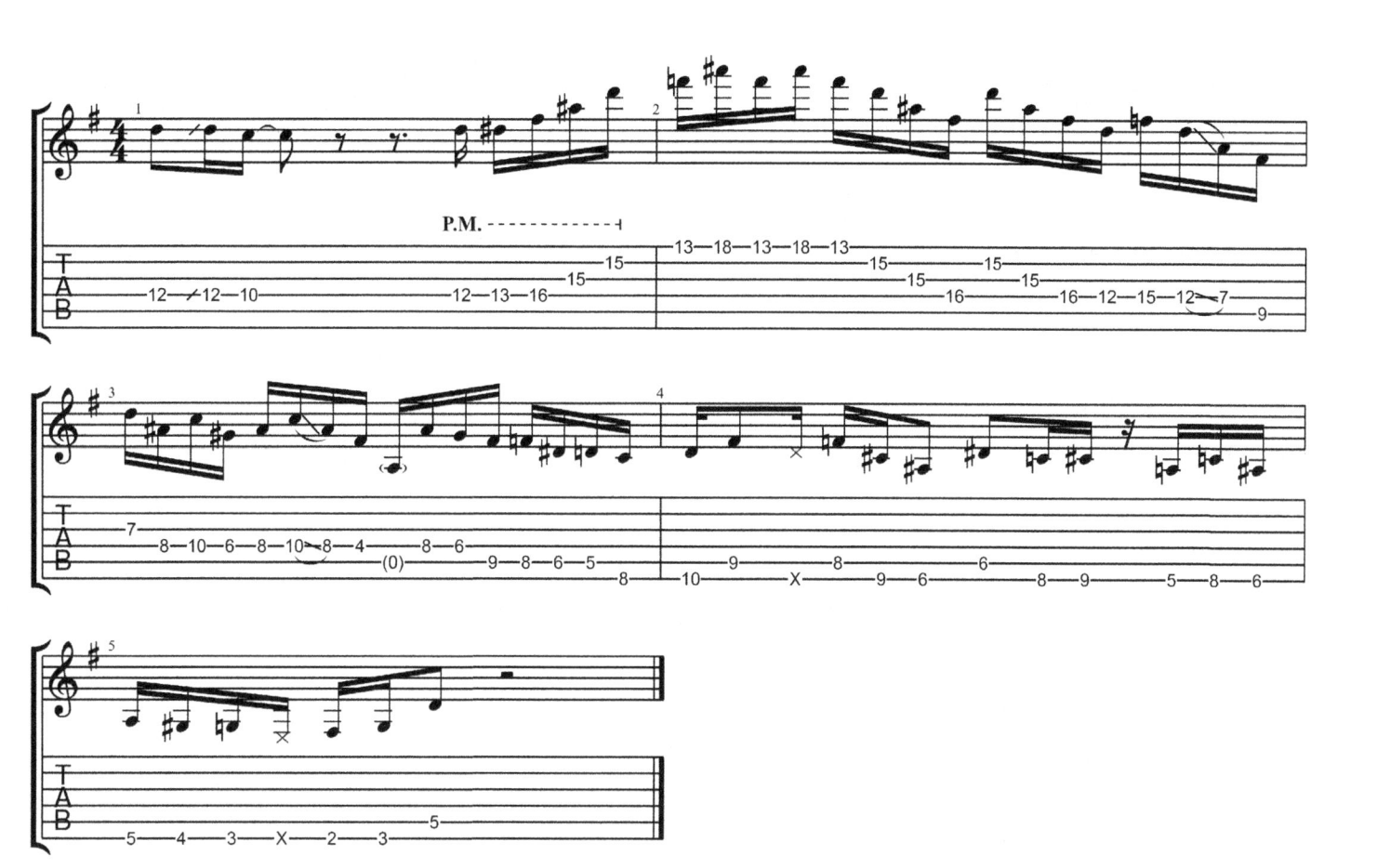

In the next lick, after the bluesy bends we move into a descending run that begins with an intervallic idea. The lick in bar three is introduced with four notes from the D Mixolydian scale followed by a pedal tone idea where the #5 note from D Altered is referenced several times to imply a D7#5 harmony. The rest of this line combines notes from D Mixolydian and D Altered.

Example 4q

The next lick begins with a dramatic run that rapidly spans the range of the neck. This is a challenging lick, so to get it sounding smooth, first combine the two 1/16th note triplet phrases and play them legato, hammering on the notes from the open strings.

To play the four-note 1/32nd phrase, I suggest holding down the last three notes of the phrase as a small chord shape. Play the G note (D string, fret 5) then slide up one fret into the chord shape to play the remaining three notes. From there, you should be able to jump to the A# note on the high E string and execute the fast slide all the way up to fret 17. The rest of this line features some more standard blues vocabulary.

Example 4r

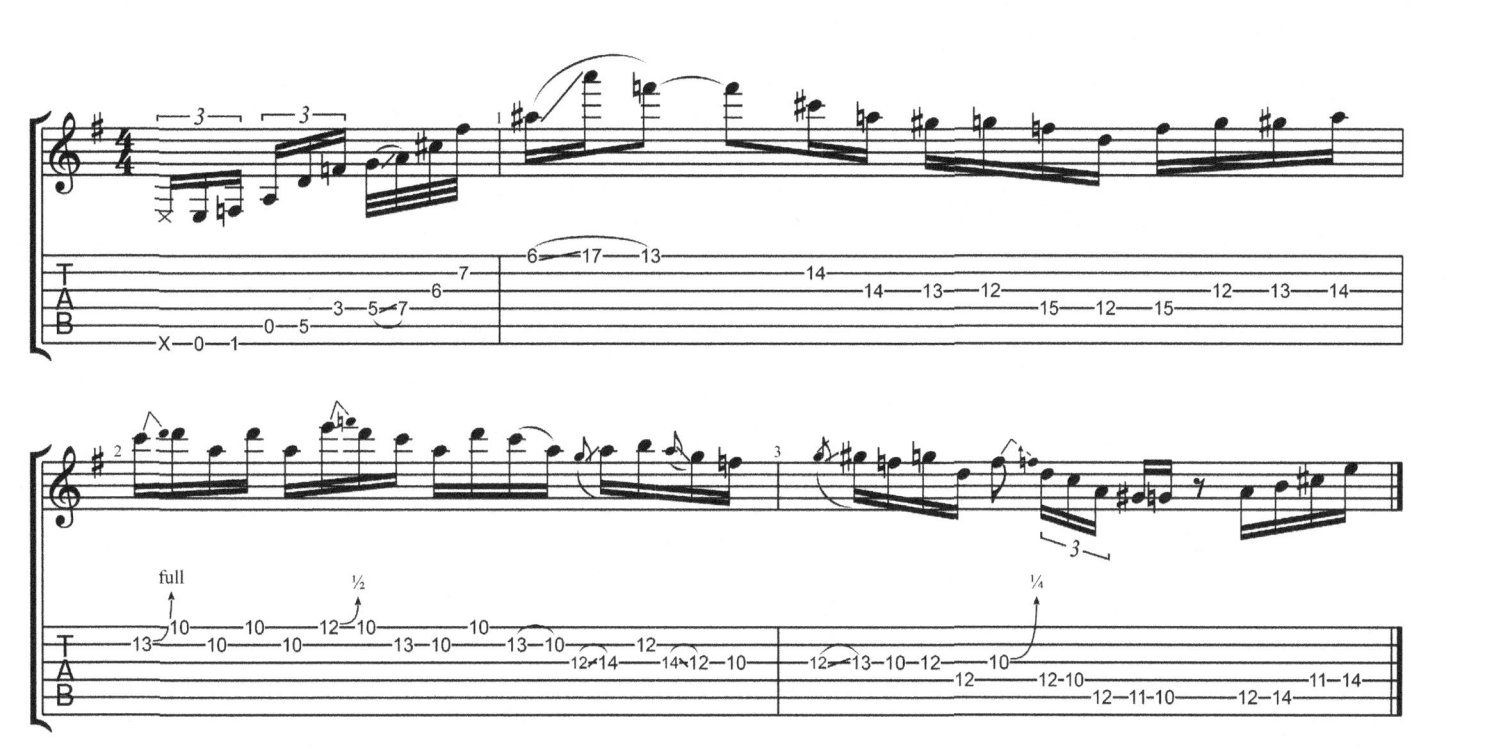

Next up is a 1/16th note run. In bar one, the majority of the notes come from the D Mixolydian scale, but as the line transitions into bar two it is punctuated with D Altered notes and an occasional chromatic passing note.

In bar three, the phrase beginning on beat "2&" spells an Ebm(Maj7) arpeggio. Remember our table of D Altered arpeggio choices? Ebm(Maj7) is chord ii of the harmonized scale and over the D7 vamp highlights the 3rd of D7, plus #5 and b9 altered color tones.

Example 4s

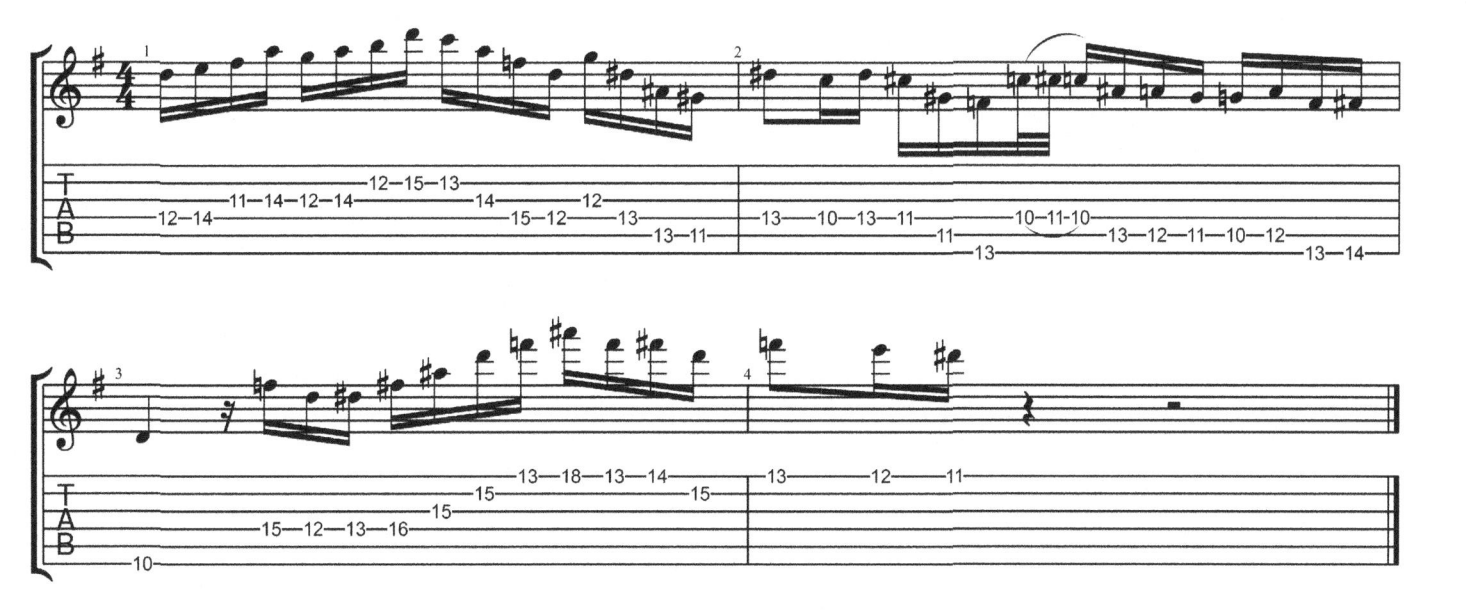

87

Here's a line that begins and ends with some blues vocabulary and adds a sequenced D Altered lick in the middle. The descending line in bar three includes three triads from the D Altered scale (Eb minor, D diminished, Gb augmented) as well as an Eb major triad that just fell under the fingers.

During your practice times, it's worth revisiting the table of triads illustrated earlier and experimenting to see how they can be combined to create short melodic phrases. Triads are very stable harmonic structures and will sound "grounded", even if they contain altered notes.

Example 4t

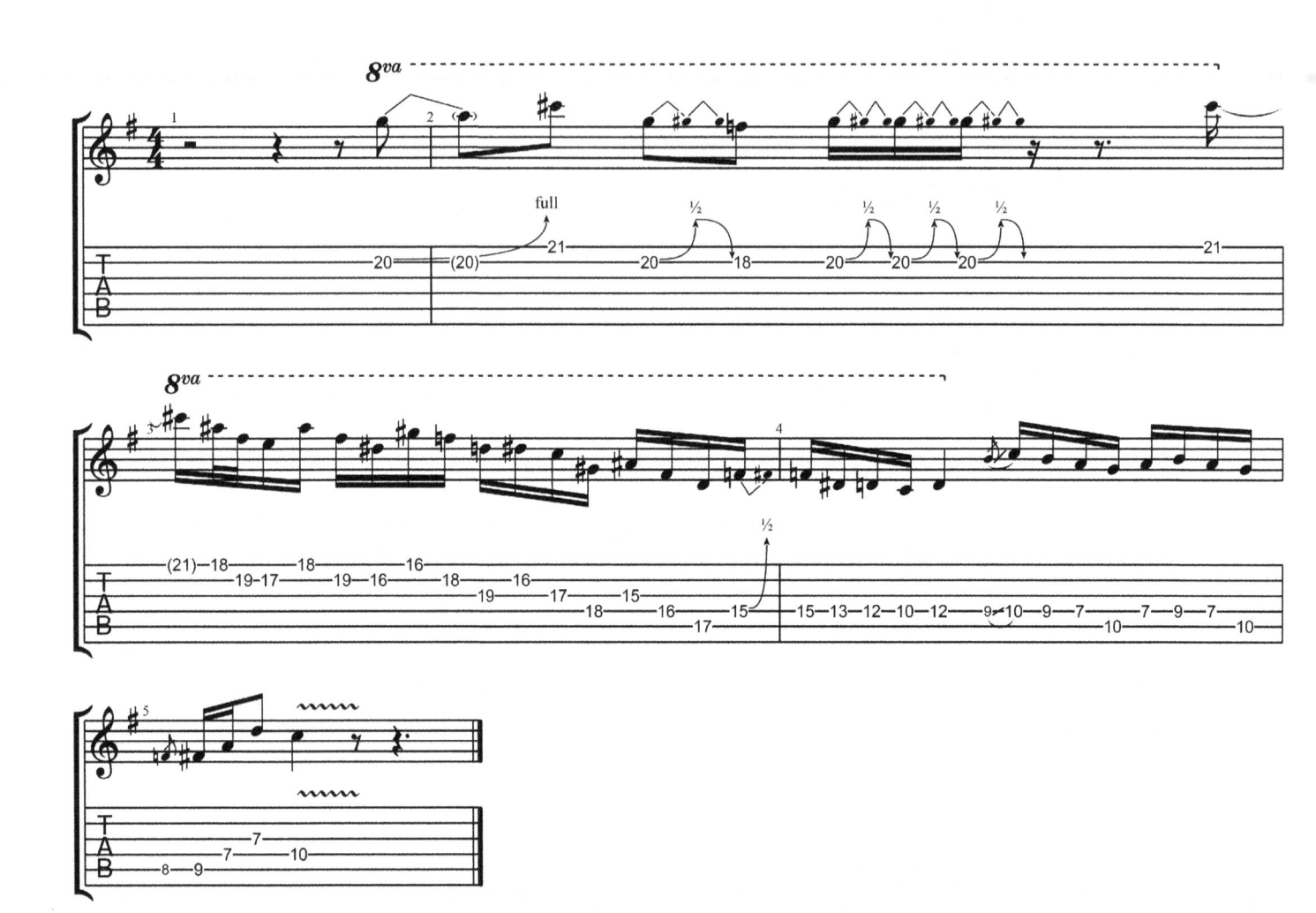

Example 4u is another example of the sidestepping technique mentioned earlier in the book. It begins with an inside sounding D minor pentatonic blues idea. By shifting this pentatonic language up a half step, we access Eb minor pentatonic. This is a simple movement on guitar and provides an easy way to get into Eb melodic minor territory (remembering that D Altered is the seventh mode of the Eb Melodic Minor parent scale). Here, the altered tension notes begin to fall under the fingers. Only one note of Eb minor pentatonic (Db, written as C#) doesn't belong to Eb Melodic Minor, but I correct this to a C natural towards the end of the bar, bringing me back inside.

Example 4u

As we head into the last phase of the solo, here is a straight-ahead blues lick. This inside-sounding phrase provides a contrast to the altered lick that will follow on from it. The descending pentatonic run at the end uses different combinations of note grouping to create a syncopated, unpredictable line.

89

Example 4v

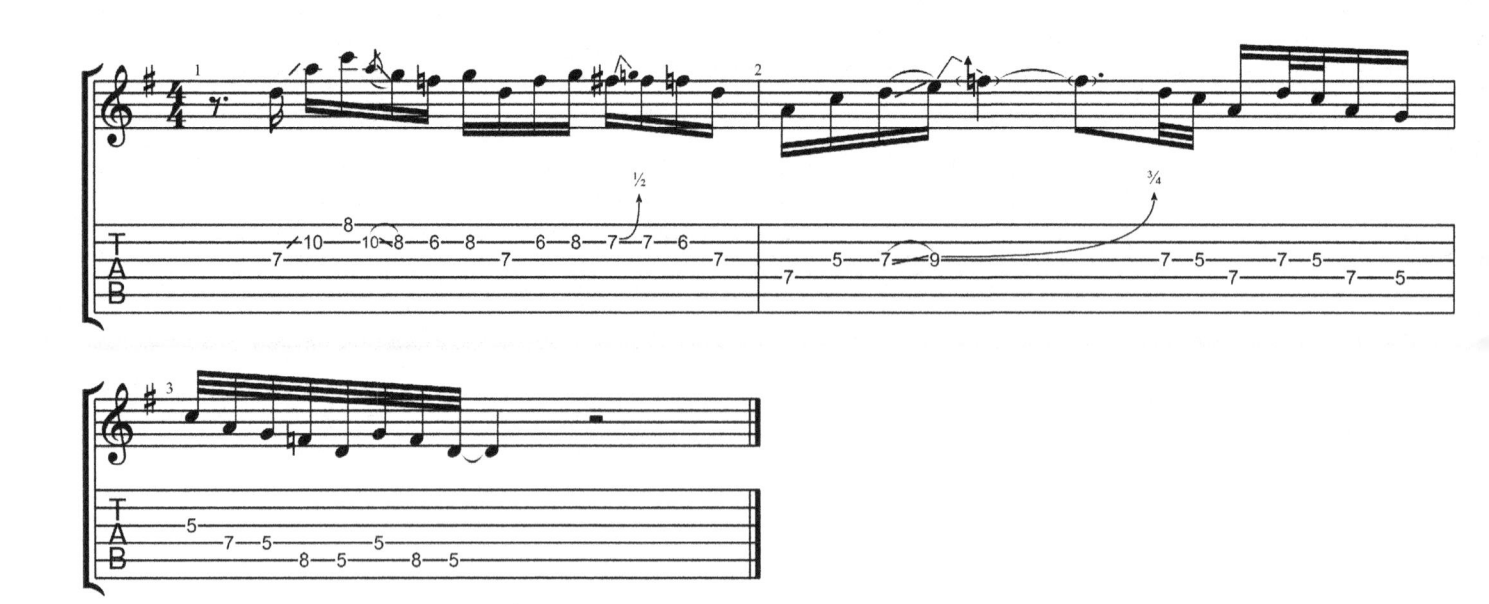

Lastly, here is an arpeggio-driven lick that moves from altered territory back into the blues.

In bar two, the first and third of the four-note phrases are arpeggios from the D Altered scale – Ebm(Maj7) and Ab major respectively.

In the second and fourth phrases, I focus on the underlying D7 chord and add tension notes. In the second phrase, the G and D# notes create a D7sus(b9) sound. In the fourth phrase, D# and F notes emphasize the b9 and #9 respectively.

Example 4w

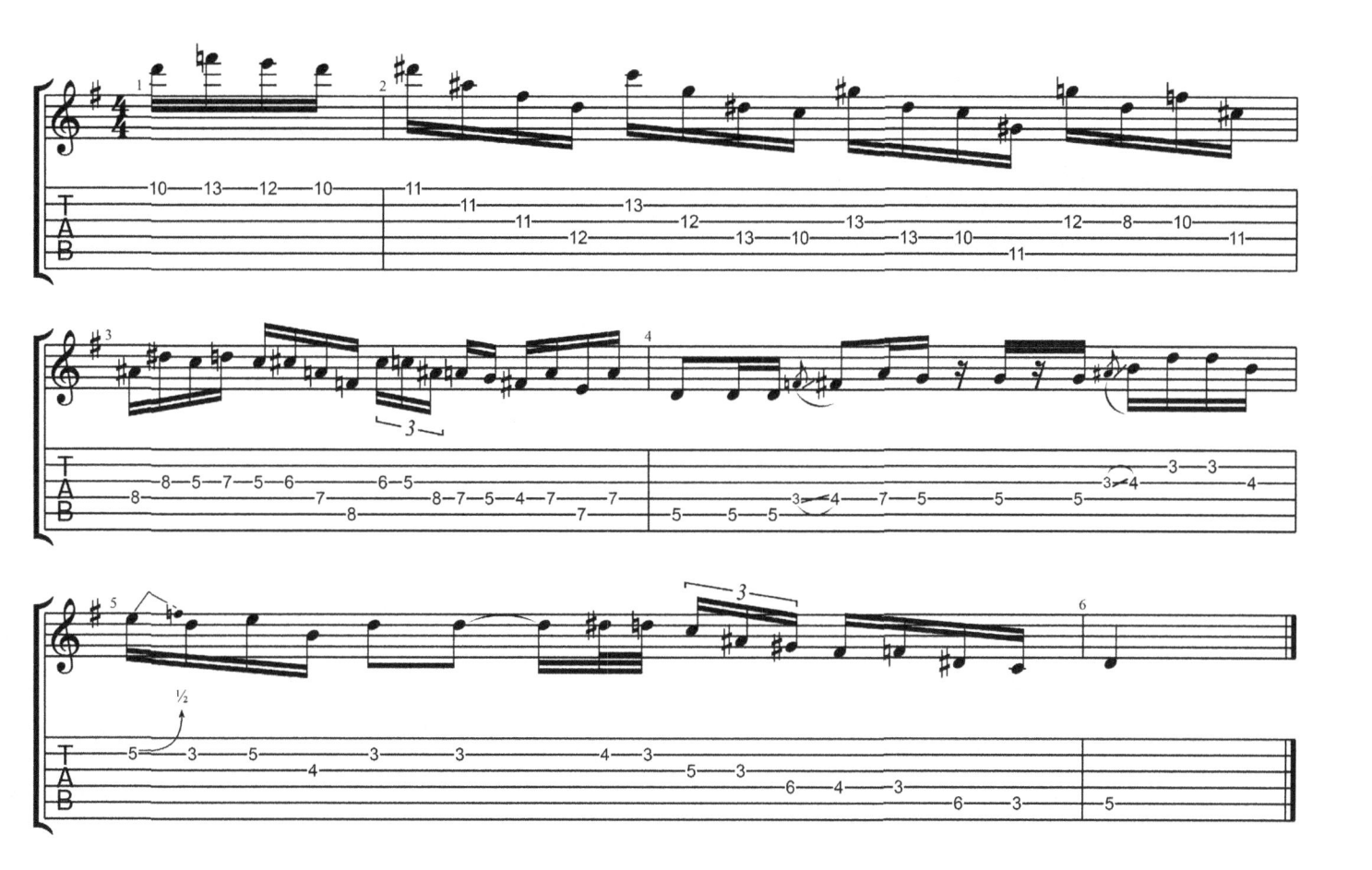

We've now covered every section of the Altered solo, so listen to the audio of the complete performance to hear how these lines link together to form the full performance. As before, connect together complete phrases until each melodic idea flows into the next.

Once you have all the fingering and position shifts down, focus on musicality and really making things groove. If you find parts of the solo tricky, focus on just those bars for a while and slow things right down, as it's important to lock the movements into muscle memory. Once that's done you will soon speed things up and play cleanly.

Play the solo along with me, using the audio track, then use this chapter's backing track to play it on your own.

Example 4x

92

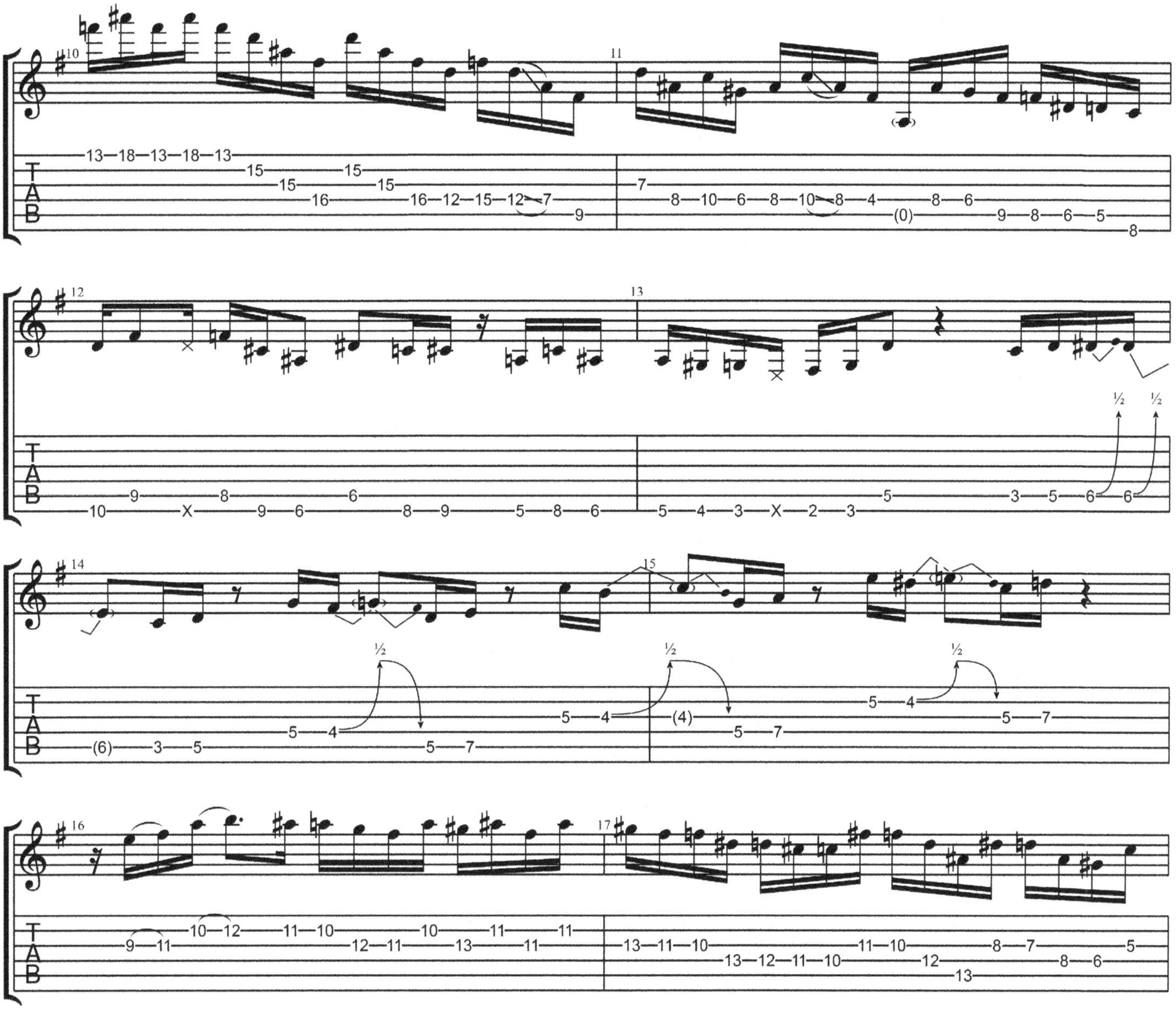

94

95

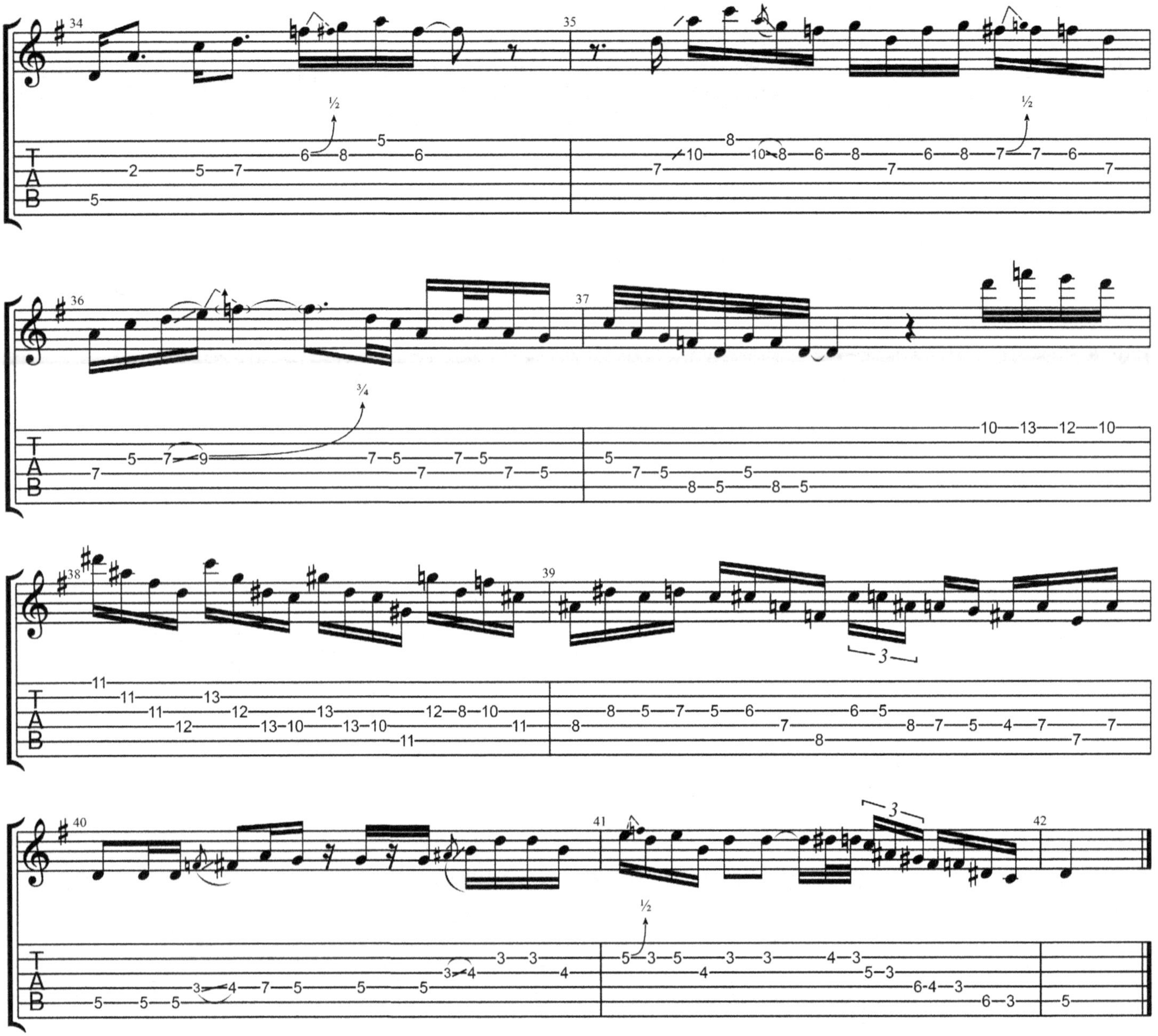

Chapter Five – Blending Scale Colors

To complete our study of inside-outside scale colors, I decided to improvise a longer solo over an up-tempo blues in the key of D Major. The underlying harmony is very simple – it sticks to the three-chord blues sequence and there are no unusual jazz changes or substitutions thrown in. Keeping the harmony simple really helps to highlight the effect that the altered scales have when played over it. It's much easier to hear the tension and resolution in the music.

My aim here was to play an engaging solo that went on a journey and developed various motifs. The music must always come first! The second goal was to mix up and blend together all the altered scale colors we've studied in this book. Note that I wasn't thinking, *Now I must play D Half-Whole Diminished over the D9 chord…* because overthinking the application of musical ideas often results in a weak or contrived performance.

The more you listen to these altered scales, the more you will absorb their sound. And the more time you spend practicing and working with these scale ideas, the more they will simply emerge naturally in your playing.

I'm not going to give you a blow by blow account of which scale I used where in this piece, but as you study the lines, see if you can identify some of the intervallic patterns we've worked through in previous chapters.

As always, break this solo down into manageable chunks. Look to see where I've taken a breath in the solo, completing one idea before moving onto the next.

Remember that it's helpful to learn a complete phrase that has a beginning, a middle, and an end. Don't be constrained by the bar lines – most of my phrases span bars.

Also, don't forget that you can practice all the ideas you've learnt over the backing tracks that accompany this book. Jam over the D blues track and see what ideas you can come up with.

Good luck and happy playing!

Oz

Example 5a

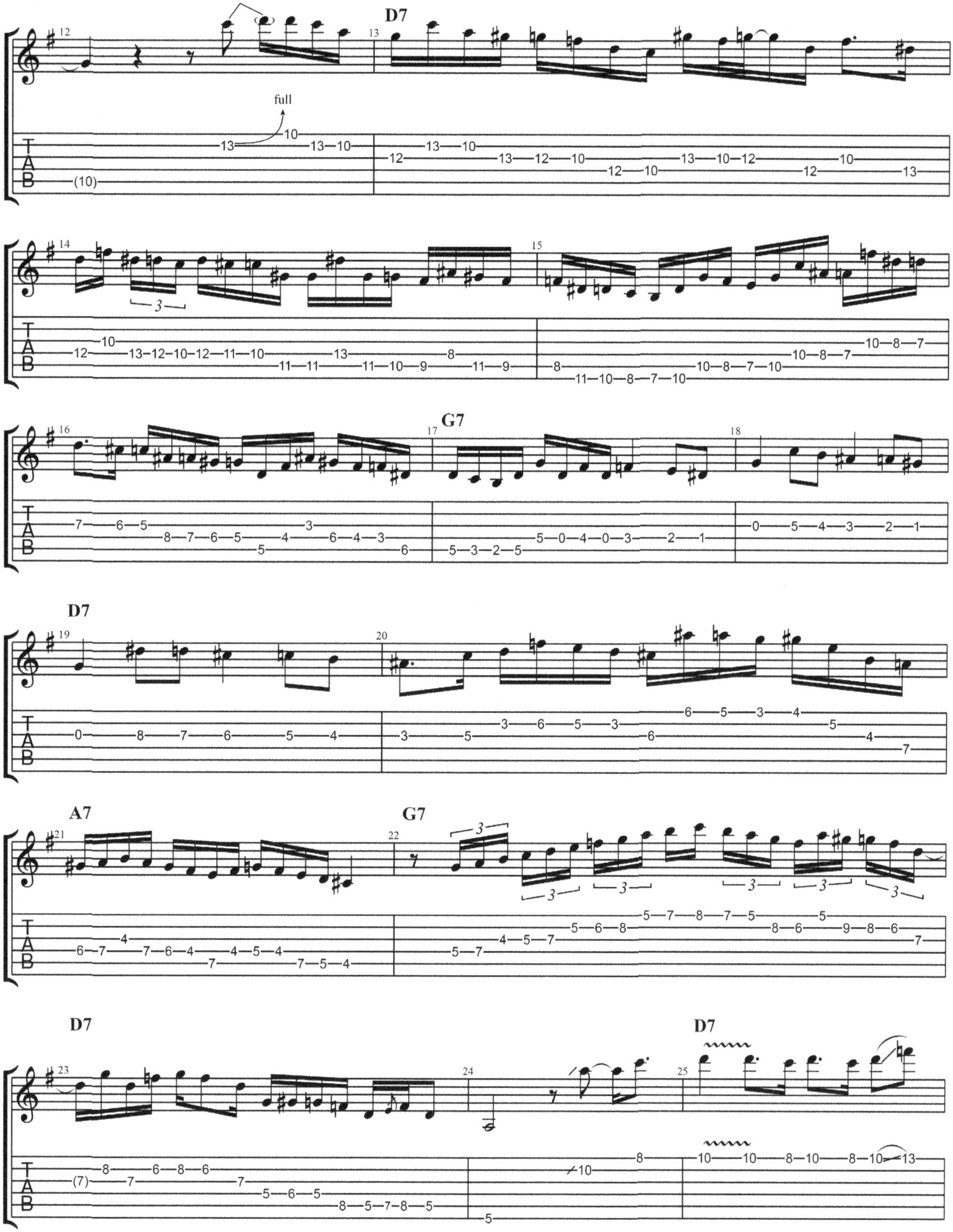
D7
full
G7
D7
A7
G7
D7
D7

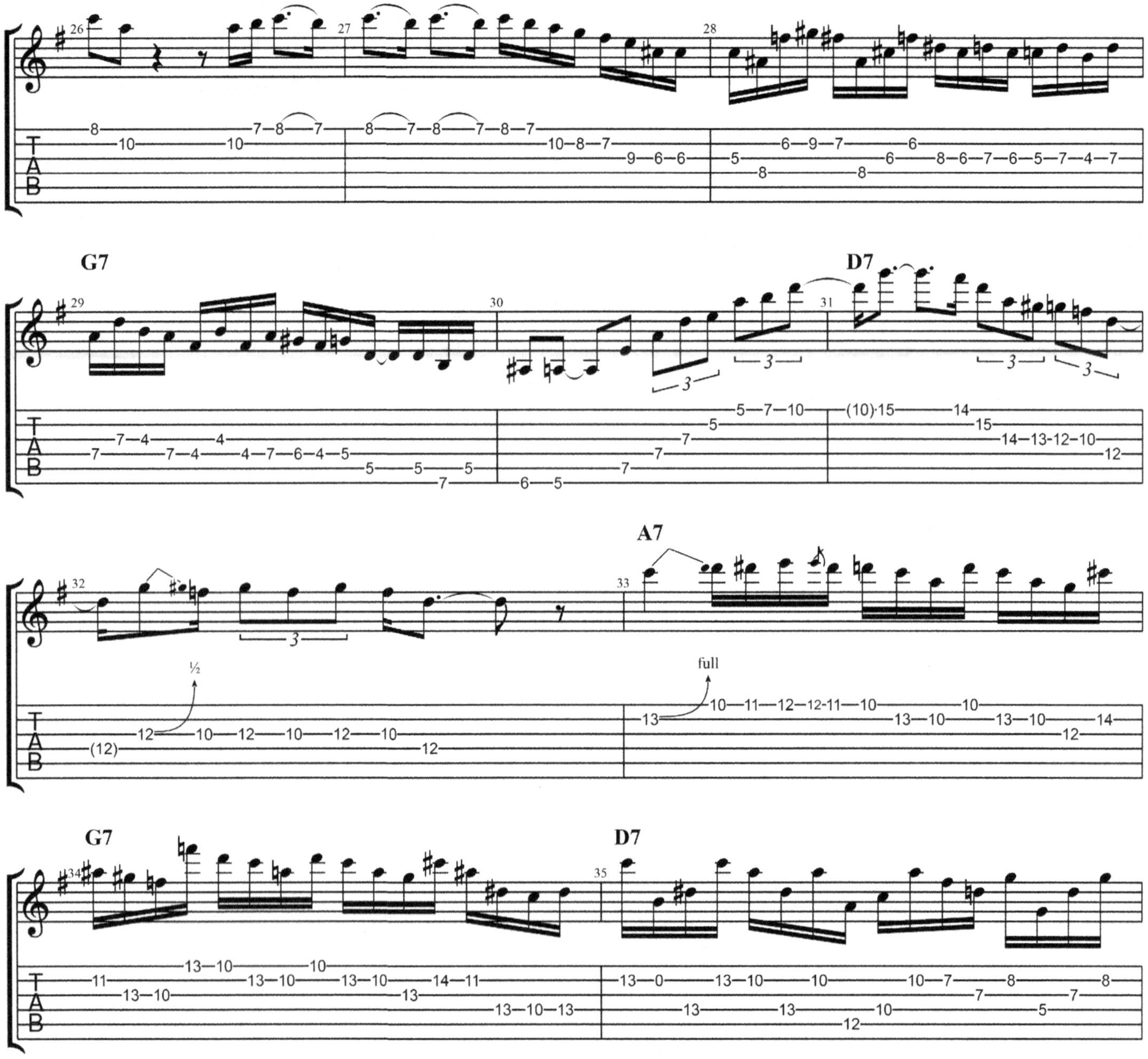
G7
D7
½
A7
full
G7
D7

101

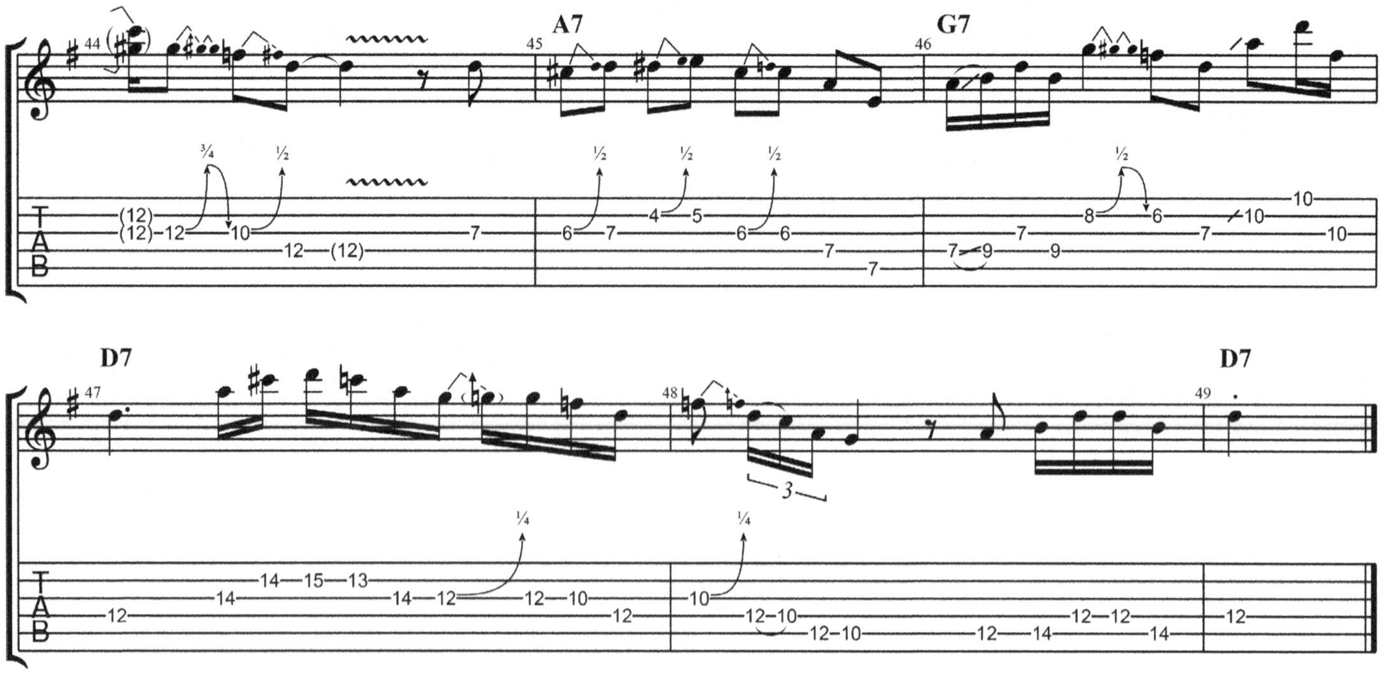
A7
G7
D7
D7